BARBARA D. INGERSOLL, Ph.D.
and SAM GOLDSTEIN, Ph.D.

Lonely, Sad
and Angry

A Parent's Guide to Depression
in Children and Adolescents

Specialty Press, Inc.
300 N.W. 70th Ave.
Plantation, Flordia 33317

ISBN 1-886941-45-9
Specialty Press edition 2001

Library of Congress Cataloging-in-Publication Data

Ingersoll, Barbara D., 1945-
    Lonely, sad and angry: a parent's guide to depression in children
    and adolescents/
    Barbara D. Ingersoll and Sam Goldstein.
        p. cm.
    Originally published: New York: Doubleday, 1995.
    Includes bibliographical references and index.
    ISBN 1-886941-45-9 (alk. paper)
        1. Depression in children--Popular works. 2. Depression in
adolescence--Popular works. I. Goldstein, Sam, 1952- II. Title.

    RJ506.D4 I54 2001
    618.92'8527--dc21   2001017033

Printed in the United States of America
Specialty Press, Inc.
300 Northwest 70th Avenue, Suite 102
Plantation, Florida 33317
(954) 792-8100 • (800) 233-9273
www.addwarehouse.com

What professionals are saying about this book!

...adolescents suffer from depression. Drs. Ingersoll and Goldstein have written an invaluable, comprehensive, compassionate resource for parents. This book will not only be of great help for parents, but for teachers and mental health professionals as well. Ingersoll and Goldstein deserve our gratitude for helping us to understand and help children who suffer from depression."
—Robert Brooks, Ph.D., Clinical Psychologist

"...should be read by parents, teachers, professionals, policy makers and all those interested in recognizing childrens' problems and helping them."
—Harold I. Eist, M.D., Past President, American Psychiatric Association

"Ingersoll and Goldstein enable parents to more confidently and intelligently recognize depression in their children, obtain proper professional help, determine appropriate treatment, cope with the daily struggles...and gain hope for a more enlightened future."
—Irene Wood, Booklist

"...valuable reference for parents..."
—Publishers Weekly

"Lonely, Sad and Angry has been welcomed by parents and psychiatrists as one of the best books on depression in the young."
—DRADA Book Committee

This work is dedicated to my father. His tireless effort and devotion to me gave my life direction. For Allyson, Janet, and Ryan, whose lives make mine richer.

S.G.

This book could not have been written without the help of my dear friend and esteemed colleague, Dr. Harold Eist. In his tireless dedication to the pursuit of knowledge and the well-being of his patients, he has set a standard toward which all who work with children might aspire.

B.D.I.

And to the hundreds of children and adolescents who have walked into our lives as patients. They have taught us to observe more closely, to listen more carefully, and to advocate more forcefully. Had we not been privileged to see so many children over the years, we would never have undertaken the task of writing this book.

B.D.I. and S.G.

Contents

Preface

OUR PURPOSE in writing this book is to provide a source of accurate and up-to-date information about depression and depressive disorders in children and adolescents. We believe that our message is an important one, since all indications are that mood disorders are much more widespread among our youth than most of us realize. We hope that parents, teachers, and others who work closely with children will find this information useful and that it will result in many more youngsters being appropriately diagnosed and successfully treated.

Although there has been a recent explosion of research into depressive disorders in children and adolescents, so far there are few black or white answers to our questions about this painful condition. As scientists, this troubles us: we would prefer to have all the information at hand before making any pronouncements or recommendations.

As clinicians, however, we recognize that the many thousands of children who suffer from depression cannot wait until all of the results have been tallied: they need our help, now. For this reason, in writing this book we have drawn upon our combined forty plus years of experience in working with troubled children and their families to supplement what we know from controlled scientific investigations. As a reader, you must recognize that this book is truly a work-in-progress: as we learn more about the mood disorders and their treatment, our suggestions and our ideas may be modified accordingly.

In Chapter 1 we describe the many guises under which depressive disorders manifest themselves in young people. Because depressed children and adolescents often have related psychiatric, learning, and behavioral problems which further complicate their lives, we have devoted Chapter 2 to an overview of these commonly associated problems and conditions.

In Chapter 3 we have outlined a practical approach to obtaining a comprehensive evaluation for parents who suspect that their child or teenager is suffering from depression. While we recognize that our approach may differ in some respects from the way in which other mental health professionals go about conducting an evaluation, we believe that the approach we describe is thorough as well as practical and efficient in terms of time and money which parents expend.

In Chapter 4 we discuss the causes—biological, experiential, and environmental—that contribute to the development of depressive illness in young people. An awareness of these forces is essential if you are to understand your child's depression and deal with it in the best way possible.

Chapter 5, which begins the section on treatment of depressive disorders, describes psychological methods of treatment. Although we have placed particular emphasis on those methods that research suggests offer the greatest promise of help, we have also included other methods of psychological intervention, such as psychodynamic psychotherapy, which have stood the test of time but for which scientific data are not yet available.

In Chapter 6 we review and discuss medications which are used to treat depression in children and adults. Because parents have many questions about the potential side effects and dangers of medication, we describe side effects and offer guidelines to help you decide when and how a trial of medication should be undertaken.

Chapter 7 is devoted to the painful subjects of adolescent

suicide and psychiatric hospitalization. While these are not situations with which most parents of depressed youngsters are confronted, we have provided information to help you recognize when emergency intervention is warranted and to assist you in making the most appropriate decisions for your youngster's care and treatment.

In Chapter 8 the focus is on what you, as parents, can do to help your depressed youngster cope with and master the demands of daily life in the family and in the community. We discuss improving relationships within the family and we explain how behavior management approaches can help with behavior problems. Since depressed children often have poor peer relations, we offer suggestions to help your child succeed socially.

In Chapter 9 we discuss how teachers can spot the warning signals of depression; how they can help depressed youngsters function better in the classroom; and how the critical tie between parents and teachers can be strengthened and maintained. Since many depressed youngsters also suffer from learning disabilities and Attention-Deficit/Hyperactivity Disorder, we review the public school system's responsibility for providing appropriate services to these children under federal law.

Finally, in Chapter 10, we summarize all that has gone before in the earlier chapters. We also offer our own ideas about what the conditions in our society might be that foster such high rates of emotional illness in our youngsters and some thoughts for where the future might take us.

Lonely, Sad and Angry

ONE

What Is Childhood Depression?

"*Kathy was such a happy baby that we nicknamed her 'Sunny.' Then, suddenly, when she was about four or so, her disposition changed. You can see it in the family pictures: from a child who always had a smile on her face, she turned into such a solemn, quiet little girl. I don't know what happened and I don't know what's wrong.*"

"*We're really at our wits' end with Jeremy. If he's not whining or complaining, he's throwing a tantrum. Nothing satisfies him; nothing is ever fair; nothing we do is enough. Sometimes he says, 'I hate my life; I wish I were dead,' and that really scares us. I just wish we could figure out what's wrong with him.*"

"*Paul was always on the quiet side, but now he's locked himself away from everyone and everything. He just stays in his room for hours, listening to that awful music or playing Dungeons and Dragons with his weird friends. Something's really wrong—I can feel it."*

"When Josh was little, he was so active that he was a real handful. The doctors told us he would outgrow it but it sure doesn't seem that way. In fact, he's so irritable and nasty now that we're really almost afraid of him. Why is he acting this way? What's wrong with him?"

WHAT'S WRONG WITH OUR CHILDREN?

ACCORDING to recent public health studies in the United States, emotional disorders are widespread in our population. During any six-month period approximately 20 percent of adults in this country—or one in five—suffer from an emotional disorder.[1] Among these disorders, depression is one of the most common.

Although poets and artists have long portrayed childhood as a happy, carefree time of life, behavioral scientists now believe that children and adolescents actually suffer from emotional disorders at rates as high as or even higher than those seen in adults. In children, as in adults, depression is among the most common of these disorders.

For many years research into childhood depression lagged far behind the efforts devoted to understanding and treating depression in adults. Some child psychologists and psychiatrists were even convinced that depression did not exist in children, since they considered children too immature to experience the pain and despair that characterize depression as we know it in adults. In fact, childhood depression could not even be officially diagnosed until 1980, when the American Psychiatric Association published the third edition of the *Diagnostic and Statistical Manual of Mental Disorders.*

Now, however, facts and figures concerning childhood depression are emerging and they are quite alarming. Within the past decade or so, mental health professionals have come to agree that children, like adults, can and do suffer from depressive illness. In fact, we now know that depression not only exists in young people; it is actually far more common than we might have imagined. We know, too, that if depression is left untreated there can be serious and far-reaching consequences. Depression can influence every aspect of a child's growth and development, and children who have suffered from one depressive episode are at risk of additional bouts of depression throughout their lives.

<h3 style="text-align:center">WHAT IS DEPRESSION?</h3>

Depression has been aptly described as a "whole-body illness"[2] because it involves changes not only in mood but in almost every other area of a child's life as well. Sleep, appetite, energy, and general health may be impaired. Physical complaints such as stomachaches and headaches are common. Because depression interferes with the ability to concentrate and to think quickly, the depressed youngster's school performance usually declines. Moodiness and emotional outbursts put a strain on relationships within the family, while friendships may suffer as the depressed youngster becomes increasingly withdrawn and isolated or aggressive and argumentative.

In adolescence, complications such as antisocial behavior often emerge and depressed youngsters are likely to have increasing difficulty in school, perhaps dropping out altogether. Many depressed teenagers also abuse drugs and alcohol. Finally, depression multiplies the risk of suicide, which is now a leading cause of death among older adolescents in this country.

THE MANY FACES OF CHILDHOOD DEPRESSION:
DIAGNOSTIC GUIDELINES

All of us have days when nothing goes right; days when everything we touch seems to fall apart. The office is in chaos and
the boss is even more of a jerk than usual. At home, the toilet
overflows, flooding the bathroom, while the children scream
and hurl invectives at each other in the background. Our
spouse is crabby; our best friend seems unusually cold and
distant; and a look in the mirror confirms that, yes, it is possible to look as bad as you feel. You wonder sometimes whether
it's worth the effort to keep putting one foot in front of the
other each day.

Children, too, have their ups and downs. In fact, childhood is a time in which emotions are intense but fleeting;
changes in mood are like quicksilver. How, then, can we dis-
tinguish between a youngster who is responding normally to
stressful life circumstances and one who is clinically depressed? Does every child who has temper tantrums or who
complains, "Nobody likes me," suffer from depression? If, in
a moment of anger, your child shrieks, "I wish I were dead,"
does that mean he is depressed and possibly suicidal? How can
you tell if your child is depressed or just "going through a
phase"?

Guidelines for diagnosing depression are outlined in the
Diagnostic and Statistical Manual of Mental Disorders, published by the American Psychiatric Association (4th ed.,
1994).[3] The purpose of this manual, known as "DSM IV," is
to provide clear descriptions of various psychiatric conditions
so that psychiatrists, psychologists, and others who diagnose
these disorders will do so in the same way, using the same
criteria.

DSM IV has come under fire because, instead of providing separate guidelines for diagnosing depressive illness in
young people, it simply offers modifications of the guidelines

used to diagnose depression in adults. Critics contend that this is a serious flaw, since depression can manifest differently at different ages and developmental stages, as we will discuss. However, although characteristic symptoms may change with age, the core symptoms of a major depressive episode are the same for children and adults. Therefore, in spite of its shortcomings, we believe that the DSM IV provides the best set of standards currently available for diagnosing depressive illnesses in children and adolescents, as well as in adults.

DSM IV divides the depressive disorders—also called "mood disorders"—into several types, with guidelines for diagnosing each type. The types most commonly seen in children are major depression and dysthymia. A third type, known as bipolar disorder, is less often seen in full-blown form before adolescence, while depressive episodes caused by physical illness (e.g., stroke, multiple sclerosis) or by substance abuse are rare in young people.

MAJOR DEPRESSION

According to DSM IV guidelines, a diagnosis of major depression must include five of the following nine symptoms. At least one of the symptoms must be either (a) depressed mood OR (b) inability to derive pleasure from previously enjoyable activities. Symptoms must also be present most of the day, nearly every day, for at least a two-week period and they must also cause significant distress or impairment in functioning.

1. **Depressed or irritable mood.** While depressed adults often describe feeling sad, blue, low, or "down in the dumps," depression in children and adolescents is just as likely to take the form of general crankiness and irritability. The depressed child is often unable to tolerate frustration and may respond to minor provocations with angry outbursts. Irritable mood is usually more apparent at home than in other settings: many depressed youngsters who are explosive at home and seem to go out of their way to pick fights with family members are

able to control themselves in school and other public settings. Some researchers believe that children whose angry feelings are pervasive and not connected with any specific environmental events are more severely depressed than those in whom anger occurs in response to specific events.[4]

Depressed or irritable mood may not be constant across the course of the day. In fact, it is quite common for mood to vary in a consistent fashion across the day, a pattern called "diurnal mood variation." In some youngsters, mood is worse in the morning and improves as the day goes on, while others experience the reverse of this pattern. As noted above, many depressed youngsters describe their mood as better in school than when they are at home.

Low mood may also be reflected in feelings of loneliness and self-pity. Depressed youngsters often complain that life is unfair or that no one loves them and it is not uncommon for a depressed child to describe his parents, teachers, siblings, and classmates as "mean."

2. Diminished interest or pleasure in all, or almost all, activities. Anhedonia, or the inability to experience pleasure, is a hallmark of depression. Depressed youngsters lose interest in activities they previously found enjoyable and often complain that everything is "boring" or "dumb." They may lose interest in their friends as well and withdraw from social activities, citing various excuses such as lack of time or not feeling well.

3. Significant weight loss or weight gain, or significant increase or decrease in appetite. This symptom, which is common among depressed adults, may not be seen as frequently in youngsters who suffer from mood disorders. While some depressed children are picky eaters who fail to make expected weight gains, others develop voracious appetites, especially for carbohydrates and junk food. Some go so far as to hoard food, sneaking bags of cookies or candy and hiding them for later consumption. Carbohydrate craving is particularly likely to occur in young people who suffer from a seasonal form of depression known as Seasonal Affective Disorder (see p. 10).

4. Insomnia, excessive sleeping, or other sleep problems.
Sleep problems are common among all depressed individuals,
children and adults alike. Some depressed youngsters lie
awake for hours, unable to fall asleep. Others may awaken
repeatedly during the night and have difficulty returning to
sleep. These youngsters, many of whom also suffer from anxiety disorders in addition to depression, cannot tolerate sleeping alone. They seek refuge in the parental bed, sometimes
even sleeping on the floor or outside the bedroom door if they
are denied a place in the bed. Still other depressed children
seem to need excessive amounts of sleep (hypersomnia): no
matter how early they go to bed, rousing them in the morning
is a major undertaking.

In depressed teenagers the sleep cycle may be completely
reversed, so that the youngster sleeps during the day and remains awake all night. This pattern, which is known as "circadian reversal," can be quite difficult to correct once it has
become well established.

Depressed children, like depressed adults, often complain
of unpleasant and frightening dreams. Many, too, find sleep to
be nonrestorative; that is, even though the child gets enough
sleep, he does not feel rested or refreshed upon awakening.

5. Physical restlessness or slowed body movements. Depression can affect the speed at which a person moves and
speaks. Some depressed youngsters seem to move in slow mo-
tion, as if they were mired in molasses. They may speak
slowly, with long pauses before responding to a question or a
request. Others may appear restless and fidgety, engaging in
pacing, wringing their hands, and fiddling nervously with their
clothes, hair, or other objects.

6. Fatigue or loss of energy. Depression seems to place a
physical burden on those afflicted, so complaints of listlessness, loss of pep, and a chronic feeling of exhaustion in both
young people and adults are common. Even small tasks may
seem overwhelming and the child may become a couch potato
who does little besides lie around the house or stare at the

television. Like diurnal mood changes, energy levels may vary predictably across the course of the day, with some depressed individuals reporting greater energy in the morning and others noting improved energy later in the day.

7. Feelings of worthlessness; excessive or inappropriate guilt. Depressed individuals of all ages usually have problems with self-esteem. Because they feel that they are not as good as everyone else, people who suffer from depression may be hesitant to enter into new activities and be excessively critical of their own performance when they do so. When forced to do so, they may adopt a self-protective "I don't care" attitude. They are likely to be particularly sensitive to even mild criticism from others and to brood over any slight, no matter how small. Failure at any task, however insignificant, is catastrophic—proof that they are doomed to fail in any and all endeavors.

In fact, as we shall discuss, depressed people have an uncanny ability to view all aspects of life through mud-colored lenses. The glass they hold is never half full—it's always half empty. They consistently evaluate themselves and their world in negative terms. In their appraisal, their successes are minimized, while their failures are magnified.

Depressed youngsters may also feel exaggerated guilt over minor failings and express the belief that they should be severely punished for their misdeeds. Sometimes these guilty feelings reach extreme proportions and the child assumes personal responsibility for events he could not possibly have caused.

8. Diminished ability to think, concentrate, or make decisions. Depressed youngsters usually have problems with attention and concentration. Just as their bodily movements may be slow in tempo, their thinking may also be slowed, so it is not surprising that school performance is adversely affected. A child or adolescent who suffers from depression may also have great difficulty with decision making, turning to parents or other adults for help with even simple decisions.

9. **Recurrent thoughts of death or suicide, or a suicide plan or attempt.** Depressed children may become preoccupied with thoughts of death and dying. They may ask repeated questions about what happens to people when they die and they may express the fear that their parents, playmates, or siblings might die or be killed. In adolescents, there may be a fascination with music and literature with morbid themes. Thoughts of suicide can occur in children of all ages, but it is usually not until the teen years that depressed youngsters develop, and sometimes act upon, specific plans to kill themselves (see Chapter 7). When preadolescent children do try to kill themselves, they often employ brutal methods, such as hanging or flinging themselves in front of trains.

SUBTYPES AND ASSOCIATED FEATURES. According to DSM IV, an episode of major depression should be diagnosed if symptoms of depression persist for at least two weeks. Major depressive episodes can be classified as mild, moderate, or severe and they can occur singly or in a recurrent pattern. Depressive episodes are also categorized as occurring with or without accompanying psychotic features; that is, hallucinations or delusions. An hallucination is a false sensory perception—the person sees, hears, or smells things that aren't there. A delusion is a false belief which is firmly held in spite of convincing evidence to the contrary, such as the belief that one has superhuman powers or that one is being controlled by creatures from outer space. Some research indicates that auditory hallucinations (usually a single voice talking to the child) are fairly common in younger children who suffer from depression. Delusions, however, are rare and, when they occur, they may indicate that the youngster suffers from bipolar disorder rather than major depression.

In addition to the nine symptoms listed above, other symptoms which are commonly seen in depressed youths include significant anxiety, and excessive brooding and worrying. Some youngsters develop severe, unreasonable fears and phobias; others may actually suffer from anxiety attacks characterized by feelings of overwhelming dread and physical symptoms such as trembling, sweating, and racing heart rate. In fact, there is a considerable overlap between mood and anxiety disorders, with coexistence of the two often the rule rather than the exception. We will discuss this in more detail in Chapter 2.

Finally, some youngsters suffer from a seasonal form of depression known as Seasonal Affective Disorder, the acronym for which is SAD. These individuals suffer from annually recurring episodes of depression during the winter months, with a return to normal mood during spring and summer. Children and adults who suffer from SAD most commonly experience depression characterized by fatigue, lethargy, excessive sleeping, and increased appetite, especially for carbohydrates and junk food. Like bears, they almost seem to go into hibernation during the winter; indeed, many people who have seasonal depression have used this analogy to describe themselves in their winter state. Dr. Norman Rosenthal, director of Light Therapy Studies at the National Institute of Mental Health, notes that SAD is difficult to diagnose in young people because it takes several years for a seasonal pattern to emerge clearly and the child's problems are usually attributed to other causes.[5]

DYSTHYMIA

The word "dysthymia" (dis-thim'-e-a) comes from the Greek prefix *dys,* meaning bad, difficult, painful, or disordered, and *thymos,* which means mind. As the term is used in DSM IV, it refers to a milder form of depressive illness in which the symptoms are not as severe as those seen in major depression, although they may last longer.

For children and adolescents, a diagnosis of dysthymia must include depressed or irritable mood for most of the day, occurring more days than not, for a period of at least one year (two years for adults). During this period, there can be no more than two months in which symptoms are not present. In addition, at least two of the following symptoms must be present during this time period.

• Poor appetite or overeating

• Insomnia or excessive sleeping

• Low energy, fatigue

• Low self-esteem

• Poor concentration, difficulty making decisions

• Feelings of hopelessness

If we compare these symptoms with those seen in major depression, we see that, unlike depression, dysthymia is **not** characterized by a marked loss of pleasure or social withdrawal. Guilt and morbid preoccupation are also not part of the syndrome of dysthymia. Instead, as researchers at the University of Pittsburgh have observed, dysthymia "is predominantly characterized by gloomy and depressed mood, brooding about feeling unloved . . . irritability and anger . . . [and] self-deprecation or negative self-esteem."[6] In children, these researchers note, poor appetite and sleep problems are not very common symptoms. Instead, disobedient behavior is the most prevalent feature associated with dysthymic disorder.

Dysthymia often seems to develop as a consequence of a preexisting, chronic condition, such as Attention-Deficit/ Hyperactivity Disorder, an eating disorder, an anxiety disorder, or rheumatoid arthritis. Dysthymia usually begins in childhood, adolescence, or early adult life and persists for many years. In fact, it has often been referred to as "depressive personality," since depressive symptoms are so longstanding and so deeply ingrained that they seem to become personality traits. If, as often happens, a depressive episode is subsequently superimposed on an existing dysthymic disorder, this is known as "double depression."

Dr. Harold Eist, a gifted and experienced child psychiatrist in the Washington, D.C., area, puts it succinctly when he states, "Dysthymia keeps youngsters chronically poised on the brink of depression." In fact, we find that the vast majority of youngsters with dysthymia eventually develop major depression. Many of these youngsters then go on to have recurrent episodes of depression or bipolar illness.[7] Often, in such individuals, dysthymia persists after recovery from major depression, so that the person is never really completely free of symptoms. In addition, individuals who suffer from double depression are more likely than those with depression alone to have recurrent episodes of major depression.[8]

Thus, while dysthymia is less severe and incapacitating than major depression, it is by no means a negligible or minor problem since, in addition to the suffering it causes, it usually portends greater problems to come. The hope is that, since dysthymia often predates the appearance of depression by as much as three years, if it is promptly identified and treated, major depressive episodes might be delayed or even prevented.

BIPOLAR DISORDER

Bipolar disorder, more commonly called manic-depressive disorder, is a condition characterized by depressive episodes interspersed with periods in which mood and energy are excessively elevated—elevated, in fact, well beyond normal levels of a good mood. When people who suffer from manic-depressive disorder are in a manic phase, they don't just feel good: they feel GREAT. In such an expansive mood, they enthusiastically seek the company of others and fling themselves into all sorts of activities, without regard for the consequences. Although elevated mood is considered to be the core symptom of mania, in some individuals the mood disturbance takes the form of irritability, which is most apparent when the person is thwarted.

DSM IV describes a manic episode as "a period of abnormally and persistently elevated, expansive, or irritable mood" in which at least three of the following symptoms are present.

1. **Inflated self-esteem or grandiosity.** When people who have manic-depressive illness are in a manic phase, they may have very exaggerated notions of their own importance or abilities. These notions can range from the erroneous belief that they have special knowledge or talents to delusional beliefs that they are divine messengers from God or the reembodiment of a famous person such as Christ or Napoleon. They are boastful and bubbling over with self-confidence and they may begin vast projects for which they have no special talent or give advice on subjects about which they have no particular knowledge. In children, outspoken oppositional behavior and direct challenges to authority may be a form of grandiosity or exaggerated notions of their omnipotence and may, therefore, be indicative of a manic or hypomanic state.

2. **Decreased need for sleep.** In a manic state, people often have greatly reduced need for sleep, sometimes even going for days at a time without sleep with no apparent loss of energy.

3. **More talkative than usual or pressured speech.** Manic speech is usually loud, rapid, and difficult to interrupt. In a manic phase, the person's conversation is usually punctuated by jokes, puns, and plays on words. If the manic person's mood is irritable instead of elevated, he may be quite argumentative or spout complaints, insults, and hostile comments with very little provocation.

4. **Jumping from one subject to another without obvious connections ("flight of ideas") or the feeling that thoughts are racing too fast.** In a manic phase, people flit from idea to idea so rapidly that it is difficult or impossible for others to follow their train of thought.

5. **Distractibility.** As we might suspect from the foregoing symptoms, manic individuals are easily distracted by irrelevant things like background noise or pictures on the wall. They can never stay on any topic for very long before something else attracts their attention.

6. **Increased activity at work, school, or socially.** Manic people have so much energy and such a flood of ideas that they may throw themselves into all sorts of activities, sometimes in a very disorganized and chaotic way. While some mildly afflicted individuals can be highly creative during manic episodes, those who are more severely impaired involve themselves in activities that have disastrous social, professional, or financial repercussions. As noted above, there is almost always increased "people-seeking" behavior and, not recognizing the inappropriateness of their actions, they may intrude on others in all sorts of ways, including middle-of-the-night phone calls or unannounced visits at odd hours.

7. **Involvement in impulsive behavior with the potential for painful consequences.** Manic individuals are prone to engage in all sorts of high-risk activities, from driving recklessly to squandering all of their money on buying sprees or foolish business investments. A manic teenager might begin to engage in sexually promiscuous behavior or suddenly decide to abscond with the family car on a cross-country joy ride. Many manic teenagers further complicate their condition by binge drinking and use of illegal drugs.

ASSOCIATED FEATURES. Manic episodes usually begin quite suddenly and last from a few days to a few months. While in a manic phase, the person often does not realize that he is behaving strangely and may resist all attempts to provide treatment. It is common, too, to see abrupt changes in mood, with rapid shifts from euphoria to anger or depression. The manic teenager typically refuses to abide by longstanding rules and may blatantly flout authority. Emotional reactions are extreme, and things are seen as either completely good or completely bad, with very few "gray areas."

Bipolar illness is often difficult to diagnose before the teen years. We know, however, that one in four children who suffer from major depression will eventually develop bipolar illness.[9] Those who are at greatest risk include youngsters with a history of severe hyperactivity, temper outbursts, and unstable mood as well as a family history of bipolar illness and alcoholism.[10] In comparison with depressed adolescents who do not go on to develop manic-depressive illness, those who do are characterized by an earlier age of onset of their depression and their depressive episodes are usually sudden in onset and include psychotic symptoms, excessive sleeping, and slowed motor activity.[11]

THROUGH THE YEARS: DEPRESSION
ACROSS THE LIFE SPAN

INFANCY

In a voice breaking with emotion, Michelle's mother said plaintively, "I don't understand what's happened to my daughter. She was such a great baby—so bouncy, so much fun. And now look at her: she's really a different child."

As a newborn, Michelle was indeed the ideal baby in every respect. Blessed with a pleasant disposition, she was happy, healthy, and alert. By two months of age she was sleeping through the night and had settled easily into predictable routines. She nursed well, seemed closely attached to both parents, and responded to parental attention and affection with broad smiles and excited chortles.

When Michelle was six months old, however, her world suddenly changed. Her mother developed an acute illness that required bed rest and repeated hospitalizations. Breast feeding was abruptly discontinued when Michelle's mother entered the hospital for the first time for a two-week stay. During that time an aunt took care of Michelle while her father spent long hours in the hospital at his wife's bedside.

Within two months, Michelle seemed like a different child. Her sunny disposition vanished and she became fussy, irritable, and difficult to soothe. Her appetite waned and, instead of making expected weight gains, she actually lost weight.

When Michelle's mother returned from her last hospital stay, the happy baby she had left behind had changed unmistakably. She greeted her mother without enthusiasm and seemed unresponsive to any attempts to catch her interest or engage her in play. Gone were the smiles and the chuckles, replaced by a downcast expression which suggested that Michelle was a very sad little child indeed.

Can babies be depressed? As difficult as it is to accept the idea that children can suffer from mood disorders, it's almost mind-boggling to think that infants and toddlers can be depressed. Yet there is good evidence that infants as young as a few weeks of age can and do suffer from depression.

During the first year of life, depressive disorders reflect problems with attachment and mothering. In some cases, like that of Michelle described above, the mother-child bond is broken by illness, death, or separation for other reasons. Almost fifty years ago psychoanalyst René Spitz described a syndrome of depressive symptoms in institutionalized infants separated from their mothers.[12] This syndrome, which he called "anaclitic depression," was characterized by retarded development, weepiness, apathy and withdrawal, poor appetite and weight loss, and sleep disturbances. If separation from the mother or other primary caregiver lasted less than three to five months, most infants recovered. However, if separation continued beyond this point, the symptoms worsened dramatically and many of the children actually died within the first year.

Actual physical separation from the mother or other primary caregiver is not necessary for young children to develop symptoms which would constitute evidence of depression in an adult. In some cases the child's symptoms can develop as a result of simple neglect. For example, a single parent who lacks family support and other resources may be so overwhelmed by the demands of daily life that he or she is too exhausted to give the child more than the most perfunctory care. Parents who are addicted to drugs or alcohol or who suffer from severe depression may be so irritable, withdrawn, or preoccupied with their own problems that they cannot meet the infant's basic physical and emotional needs. The infant, then, cannot successfully move on to the next developmental stage.

THE PRESCHOOL YEARS

Four-year-old David had never been an easy child. As an infant, he was fussy and difficult to comfort and, as a toddler, tantrums and outbursts often occurred with little provocation. As his mother explained to the child psychiatrist, "He's always been a screamer—the least little thing could set him off." His mother also reported that toilet training was a particularly difficult struggle: although David was willing to use the potty for urination, he resisted using the potty for bowel movements. Instead, he often crouched in a corner or hid behind a piece of furniture to have a bowel movement in his diaper.

David entered preschool at age three and, after some initial protests at being separated from his mother, he seemed to make a good adjustment. Just before his fourth birthday, however, his father abandoned the family, moved in with another woman, and filed for divorce. In the weeks that followed, David became increasingly oppositional and aggressive at home. His anger spilled over into the nursery school setting, where he was often in the time-out chair for misbehavior. When he regressed in his toileting behavior and began to soil his underpants, his mother recognized his distress and sought professional help.

Depressed preschoolers are often sulky and uncoopera-
tive, with frequent crying spells and temper tantrums. The depressed preschool child may have a sad appearance as well as
sleep and appetite problems. Separation anxiety and a tendency to withdraw from other children can make adjustment
to nursery school problematic for some depressed youngsters,
while others encounter difficulties due to aggressive and defiant behavior.

What causes a youngster in this age group to become
depressed? Researchers have found that many of these children are victims of abuse and neglect.[13] Other depressed
preschoolers have experienced different kinds of traumatic or
stressful events, such as parental divorce or serious illness in
themselves or a close family member. In some very vulnerable
youngsters, symptoms of depression first appear following the
birth of a sibling, when the youngster must share his parents'
attention with an unwelcome intruder. Sometimes this antipa-
thy persists and we find the depressed child or adolescent still
consumed with resentment of his younger brother or sister
many years later.

MIDDLE CHILDHOOD

*The well-dressed couple in the psychologist's office
seemed uncertain as to how to begin. After a moment, it
was the husband who spoke. "Doctor, my wife and I
don't agree about what's going on with our daughter. My
wife thinks that Elizabeth has some kind of emotional
problem but I don't agree. I think we've just spoiled Elizabeth rotten and now she's out of control. She's so lazy
that it's unbelievable and her temper is just awful. If
somebody looks at her the wrong way—especially if that
somebody is her brother—she blows up and has a fit." He
paused for a moment and looked perplexed. "You know,
Elizabeth and her brother used to get along pretty well.
But now, if they're in the same room together, you'd*

swear it was World War III. Last summer we were out one night and they got into such a screaming match that the neighbors called the police."

Again he paused and turned to his wife. In a troubled voice she said, "I agree that Elizabeth is having problems but I don't think that she is lazy or spoiled. Before all this started she was always a pretty good kid. I could count on her to do little chores around the house and to keep an eye on her brother for me. Now she really seems to hate her brother—I agree with Jim on that. And she doesn't do much with her friends now, although she used to be a pretty popular kid. She's always so angry and so unhappy: she's started saying things like 'I wish I were dead,' and 'I hate my life.' She sounds like she means it and that really scares me."

In the depressed school-age child, low mood, irritability, poor self-esteem, and an inability to have fun are often obvious to others. The child may also be preoccupied with morbid fantasies, develop a variety of fears and phobias, and withdraw from the company of others. School performance is adversely affected and some depressed youngsters refuse to go to school, often claiming illness. In fact, physical complaints, such as headaches and stomachaches, for which no organic cause can be found are seen in about 70 percent of depressed children.[14] Hallucinations, common in this age group, affect as many as one third of depressed youngsters[15] and usually consist of a single voice talking to the child.

ADOLESCENCE

Jenny, age thirteen, keeps her family in constant turmoil with her angry outbursts, rude remarks, and chronic complaints about her "miserable life" and her "rotten family."

At sixteen, Sam appears to be on "a fast train to

nowhere," according to his parents. They are appalled at his appearance, worried about his choice of friends, and upset by his poor school performance and frequent violations of rules at home and in school.

If, like so many people, you believe that these are descriptions of "typical teenagers," you are way off the mark. In reality, research over the past thirty years has consistently shown that the majority of adolescents meet the challenges of this developmental stage successfully and do not engage in extreme behavior nor do they develop an emotional disorder.[16]

Yet the idea that adolescence is inevitably a time of great emotional turmoil, mood swings, and rebelliousness has persisted, along with the belief that the young person will "outgrow" these difficulties with maturation. The unfortunate result is that many seriously depressed youngsters do not receive much-needed treatment and may then go on to have serious psychiatric problems as adults.

In teenagers, depression can manifest itself in many ways. Common symptoms include restlessness, irritability, and argumentativeness. Poor school performance is likely and many depressed adolescents develop patterns of antisocial behavior, including running away from home, stealing, sexual promiscuity, and the use of drugs and alcohol. Social withdrawal, common in depressed adults, may occur. However, while some depressed teenagers may retreat from the world and isolate themselves from friends and family, others seem obsessed with a desire to spend time with their friends, almost as if social activities were a drug which temporarily improves mood. This is baffling to parents who, when depression is diagnosed in their adolescent, protest "But he's not too depressed to talk on the phone or go out with his friends till all hours."

During adolescence we see a dramatic change in the ratio of females to males who suffer from depression, with females taking an early and enormous lead. How can we account for this sudden jump in the number of depressed adolescent girls? We don't really know the answer to this question. Some researchers have suggested that the hormonal changes which accompany puberty are responsible for higher rates of depression in adolescent girls, a notion which makes sense in light of what we know about changes in mood associated with hormonal changes during the menstrual cycle, pregnancy, and childbirth. Others speculate that males and females have different response styles in which males distract themselves from a depressed mood, whereas women ruminate and therefore amplify the depressed mood. Others believe that the reason lies in the fact that girls are treated differently from boys and face more challenges during their early teen years (e.g., girls are more likely than boys to go through puberty before or during the transition to secondary school[17]).

Depression in adolescence may come on suddenly or it may occur as an exacerbation of longstanding problems.

"Lee's never been an easy kid but he's gone from 'difficult' as a little kid to 'impossible' as a teenager. He was always hyperactive—we actually had to put a latch on his bedroom door so he couldn't wander around the house or the neighborhood in the middle of the night. He had some learning problems, too, but everything seemed to improve a lot when he started taking Ritalin and getting some special help in school. He did OK—in fact, he did great—until about a year or so ago.

"We're not sure what happened; maybe it started when his best friend moved away. They were so close and I know Lee took it hard when Jeff left. For a couple of weeks he just hung around looking down, not doing much or saying much. If you came near him or said anything to him, he'd kind of snarl. Then he started hanging out with some new friends, kids we don't like. I know they smoke; I can smell it on him. I don't know about drugs but I'm sure they drink. Lee's come home a couple

of times, acting funny and smelling like beer. He doesn't seem to care much about school anymore and his grades have gone down the tubes. When we try to talk to him about things, he just clams up and tells us to get off his back."

HOW WIDESPREAD IS THE PROBLEM?

For a condition that was not even recognized until quite recently, the statistics that are now emerging about depression in children and adolescents are alarming.* During a year's time, 8–9 percent of children between the ages of ten and thirteen suffer an episode of major depression and a typical episode lasts for almost a year. For a few years, this rate remains fairly steady for boys. For girls, however, the rate shoots up dramatically: as many as 16 percent of girls ages fourteen to sixteen are affected. By the age of eighteen, as many as one out of every five teenagers has suffered from at least one episode of major depression.[18] Through the adult years, the rate of major depression remains higher for women than for men.

Dysthymia is about half as common as major depression but an episode of dysthymia typically lasts much longer (up to five years). Dysthymia also increases the likelihood that the victim will subsequently experience a full-blown episode of major depression.[19]

To present these statistics from a slightly different perspective, let us follow a group of a thousand high school students for a period of one year. During this time approximately forty of these youngsters will suffer from an episode of depressive illness for the first time in their lives. Another thirty or so

---

* Because researchers have used different procedures to diagnose depression, statistics cited by different groups of investigators may vary. For example, research indicates that at any given time as many as 40 percent of adolescents may experience short periods of **depressed mood**. However, a much smaller number actually meet DSM IV criteria for a diagnosis of **major depression**.

will become depressed for the second or third time. This means that, during the course of a single year, approximately 7 percent of the adolescent population of this country experience an episode of depressive illness.[20]

Childhood depression is by no means just an American phenomenon. In fact, a number of studies have actually revealed a higher incidence of childhood and adolescent depression in other countries.[21]

As startling as these figures are, they reflect only the tip of the iceberg. Large-scale studies indicate that rates of depression are actually increasing rapidly in our country and abroad. For example, when we divide the population of this country into two groups—those who are under forty years of age and those who are over the age of forty—we find that those under forty are **three times** more likely to suffer from a depressive illness than those over forty.[22] What's more, if we examine the under-forty group more closely, the trend is clear: as age goes down, the risk of having a depressive illness goes up.[23]

Why is this happening? No one really knows the answer to this question, although we discuss possible contributing factors in Chapter 10. One point on which there is complete agreement, however, is that those who are at greatest risk for depressive illness are those born most recently—our children.

T W O

What Else Can Go Wrong?

Related Emotional and Behavioral Problems

COEXISTING PSYCHIATRIC CONDITIONS

IN THE PAST, mental health professionals often found themselves stymied when confronted with a youngster whose symptoms suggested the presence of more than one psychiatric condition. As clinicians, we can clearly recall lengthy discussions about such patients with our colleagues.

> *First doctor: "His mood is quite low and his self-esteem is really at rock bottom. I think he's suffering from depression."*
>
> *Second doctor: "You're right; he certainly is depressed. But you would be depressed, too, if you had to struggle in school the way he does. I think that the real problem is his learning disabilities: if they were treated, he'd be a different person."*
>
> *Third doctor: "What about his problems with atten-*

tion and concentration? Wouldn't that explain why he can't learn? And wouldn't that, in turn, make him feel bad about himself? It seems to me that the source of his problems is Attention-Deficit Disorder—everything else is just secondary to that."

And so on, and so on!

We now know, however, that with youngsters suffering from a psychiatric disorder it is usually not an "either or" situation. Children and adolescents can, and often do, suffer from two or more psychiatric disorders at the same time, a situation which is called "comorbidity." Among depressed children and adolescents, comorbidity actually appears to be the rule rather than the exception: in surveys of young people in the general population, we find that as many as half of those with depressive disorders also suffer from at least one additional psychiatric condition.[1]

If we look at young people who have been admitted to psychiatric hospitals, we see that the rates of comorbidity are even higher. Among these youngsters, the percentage of those who suffer from two or more coexisting psychiatric disorders jumps to around 80 percent.[2] This is understandable, since the presence of an additional diagnosis indicates additional symptoms and problems which, in turn, result in greater overall impairment.

For purposes of efficient communication, mental health professionals have grouped the bulk of psychiatric disorders of childhood into two broad categories. Disorders characterized by behaviors which disturb and annoy others—especially those which upset adults—are referred to as "**externalizing disorders.**" Children who are impulsive and excessively active (hyperactive) fall into this category, as do young people who seem just plain "ornery"; who, for example, seem to take particular delight in opposing and defying adult requests and directives, even when they stand to gain little or nothing by doing so. Also in this category are young people whose rule

violations are more serious—those who, for example, engage
in such antisocial activities as stealing, fighting, and abuse of
drugs and alcohol.

In contrast, youngsters who suffer from the so-called **"in-
ternalizing disorders"** are more likely to be problems to themselves than to those around them. Their problems include
withdrawn, isolated behavior, excessive anxiety, severe fears
and phobias, and, of course, depression.

ANXIETY DISORDERS

Anxiety disorders are the most prevalent form of psychiatric
illness in adults in this country.[3] They are also the most common of the psychiatric conditions which accompany depressive disorders in children. When an anxiety disorder coexists
with a mood disorder, we often find that both conditions begin quite early in life, usually before the age of twelve. Typically, the anxiety disorder appears first, before symptoms of
depression emerge. Often, too, the anxiety disorder persists
even after the youngster has recovered from depression.[4]

Children who have symptoms of both anxiety and depression usually have more family members who have psychiatric
problems than do children with depression alone.[5] Together
with such an early age of onset, this suggests that when an
anxiety disorder accompanies depression, it may be a
"marker" for a more severe form of depression. In adults, we
know that both the response to medication and the recovery
rate are better for those with an uncomplicated depression
than for those who suffer from coexisting depression and anxiety. Recent research indicates that in young people, as in
adults, a coexisting anxiety disorder increases the severity of
the depressive disorder.[6]

Anxiety disorders can take many forms but, as the term
suggests, the characteristic features are tension, worry, fear,
and apprehension. Below are descriptions of different subtypes of anxiety disorders. Bear in mind that anxiety disorders

commonly coexist with each other, as well as with depression, so a youngster who suffers from one subtype may have symptoms of one or more of the other subtypes as well.

SEPARATION ANXIETY DISORDER. At the University of Pittsburgh, Dr. Maria Kovacs and her associates are conducting a long-term study of a large group of depressed children. They have found that Separation Anxiety Disorder is the most common of the anxiety disorders which so often coexist with mood disorders.

The essential feature of this disorder is excessive anxiety about being separated from the person to whom the child is most closely attached. In most children, of course, this person is a parent, particularly the mother. Fear of separation from the mother occurs as a normal part of development in youngsters between the ages of eight and fifteen months: at this age, youngsters are expected to protest separation with tears and other signs of distress.

In older children, however, extreme anxiety concerning brief separations from familiar figures is not developmentally appropriate. Instead, it signals the existence of a psychiatric disorder.

Children with Separation Anxiety Disorder often cry, scream, tantrum, and even threaten suicide when faced with the prospect of separation from the parent. If they are forced to leave their homes or familiar areas, these youngsters become tense and fearful, especially if they have to go alone. They cannot go to visit friends, even for such a pleasurable event as a birthday party, nor can they attend sleep-overs or go to sleep-away camp. If separation is forced, these youngsters may become preoccupied with morbid fears about what might befall their parents in their absence. They become homesick almost immediately, and must often be retrieved after only a few brief hours or days away from home.

Even at home, children who suffer from Separation Anxiety Disorder are afraid to be left alone. They may shadow their parents so closely that the parent literally has no privacy, even in the bathroom: youngsters with Separation Anxiety Disorder often simply wait on the other side of the bathroom door until the parent emerges. (In children up to the age of two and a half or so, this is normal behavior: beyond that time, it is a signal that something is wrong.) These children almost always have problems sleeping alone and are frequent —if unwelcome—guests in the parental bedroom. If their parents, in desperation, deny them access, they don't return to their own beds: they just camp out outside the door to their parents' room.

In addition to their fear of separation, children with Separation Anxiety Disorder often have other fears as well. Many have intense, irrational fears (also called "phobias") of bugs, animals, and cartoon characters or people wearing costumes, such as clowns or people in Halloween getups. Medical procedures—injections, throat swabs, and the like—are particularly frightening to these children, and their extreme fear can result in wild scenes in the pediatrician's office when they must undergo such procedures.

Symptoms of Separation Anxiety Disorder can appear quite early in life; some children never seem to outgrow the normal fear of separation seen in toddlers. In other children, the onset of Separation Anxiety Disorder often follows a major change in the child's life, such as entry into school, a move, a death in the family, or a physical illness. Separation Anxiety Disorder tends to persist for many years, although there may be long periods of time when symptoms subside. As adults, many who as children suffered from this disorder continue to have problems with mood and anxiety disorders.

A common problem associated with Separation Anxiety Disorder is school refusal, sometimes called "school phobia." While most youngsters are occasionally reluctant to go to school and more than a few sometimes feign illness to enjoy a day off from school, the problem assumes epic proportions in some children, such that heroic efforts are needed every morning to pry them away from home and into school. Problems tend to be greater in the fall than the spring, and on Mondays rather than Fridays, especially after holidays or an illness requiring absence from school. With proper management, most younger school refusers return to school successfully. However, for adolescents who have a history of chronic school refusal, the outlook is somewhat guarded.[7] These youngsters may be more seriously impaired, as evidenced by the chronic nature of the problem. Conversely, chronic absenteeism may exacerbate anxiety and depression.

GENERALIZED ANXIETY DISORDER. Children with Generalized Anxiety Disorder can best be described as "worry warts." They worry about future events, like upcoming tests or social events. They worry, too, about past events, harboring guilt and self-reproach about real or imagined shortcomings in the past. Self-conscious perfectionists, they need to excel in all areas and fret constantly about what others think of them.

To an observer, these youngsters appear tense and anxious, with nervous habits like foot-tapping, nail-biting, and hair-pulling. Insomnia is usually a problem, as are complaints of stomachaches, headaches, and such anxiety-related symptoms as shortness of breath, dizziness, and nausea. Youngsters with Generalized Anxiety Disorder are often irritable, easily fatigued, and have problems with attention and concentration.

Although Separation Anxiety Disorder is the anxiety disorder most frequently seen in children who are referred to mental health professionals, some professionals believe that Generalized Anxiety Disorder may actually be more common than Separation Anxiety Disorder in the general population. Since children who suffer Generalized Anxiety Disorder are usually quiet and well behaved, their problems often go overlooked and untreated. This is particularly unfortunate, since Generalized Anxiety Disorder tends to be a chronic condition with no periods of time when the child is free of symptoms.

PHOBIC DISORDERS. Children and adolescents often experience a variety of short-lived fears as a normal part of development. Young children, for example, often express fear of animals, of the dark, and of imaginary creatures such as ghosts and monsters, while older children typically report more realistic fears, such as fear of physical danger, school failure, or loss of a loved one.

Phobias differ from normal fears in that they are more intense and distressing and tend to persist over time. Phobias which are common in the general population include fear of heights, enclosed spaces, air travel, animals, and insects. For most people, such as the city dweller who fears snakes, phobias are usually not a source of concern or inconvenience in everyday life. Phobias can be quite disabling, however, when the feared object or situation cannot be avoided (e.g., a person with an elevator phobia who works in a high-rise building or a child with a needle phobia who must undergo a blood test or receive an injection).

Social phobias—that is, fear of being in a situation in which there is a possibility of being embarrassed or humiliated in front of others—are particularly likely to interfere with a person's daily life, since one cannot always easily avoid such situations. Common types of social phobias in children and adolescents include fear of speaking or performing in front of groups, eating in the presence of others, dressing/undressing with others present, and using public bathrooms.

OBSESSIVE-COMPULSIVE DISORDER. Most of us have had the annoying experience of having a popular tune or a jingle from a television commercial repeat itself over and over in our heads. Magnify this many times over, add a distinctly frightening or unpleasant quality, and you have an obsession—a persistent thought, impulse, image, or idea which seems to be beyond the person's ability to control. The most common obsessions include repeated thoughts about becoming contaminated (e.g., by shaking hands or by touching a doorknob); repeated doubts about such things as having left a door unlocked or the stove burning; an intense need to have things in a very particular order; and impulses to do something unacceptable such as hurt one's child or shout an obscenity in church. An individual who suffers from obsessions recognizes that the thoughts are the products of his own mind and often attempts to suppress them by substituting other thoughts or actions.

Compulsions are repetitive behaviors such as hand-washing, checking, counting, and repeating words silently which the individual feels driven or "compelled" to perform to reduce the distress accompanying an obsession or to ward off some vague dread. For example, a person who obsesses about contamination may try to reduce his anxiety by scrubbing his hands until the skin is raw and bleeding.

People who suffer from Obsessive-Compulsive Disorder (OCD) know that their obsessions or compulsions are excessive and unreasonable (although children and adolescents may not always be able to make this distinction). Nevertheless, they may go to great lengths to avoid situations which involve their obsessions (for example, an individual with obsessions about contamination may avoid public rest rooms) and, in extreme cases, their avoidance may make them literally housebound. They may also spend vast amounts of time performing compulsions—so much time, in fact, that there is little left for any other activities.

Obsessive-Compulsive Disorder is relatively rare, especially among children. When it occurs, it is often seen in combination with depression or with other anxiety disorders. Although it usually begins in adolescence or the early adult years, it can also begin in childhood. Among young people with OCD, the most common obsessions are fear of contamination and thoughts of harm to self and to family members. The most common compulsions are washing, cleaning, checking, and straightening/ordering.[8]

CONDUCT DISORDER

Youngsters who qualify for a diagnosis of Conduct Disorder are those whom our parents would have called "juvenile delinquents." These are young people who bully and intimidate others; who start fights and use weapons that can cause serious physical harm; and who are deliberately cruel to people or animals. As they are described in DSM IV, young people who are diagnosed with Conduct Disorder lie, steal, violate curfew, run away from home, skip school, intentionally set fires or destroy property, and generally show a disregard for societal rules and the rights of others. Many conduct-disordered youngsters seem to have little concern for the feelings of others and show no guilt or remorse for their misdeeds.

Conduct-disordered adolescents also engage in other forms of dangerous and undesirable behavior, including smoking, drinking, and drug use. Many become sexually active at an early age and may, in fact, be quite promiscuous. Self-esteem in these youngsters is usually low, although many attempt to cover up their feelings of inadequacy with "macho" talk and behavior. Problems with academic achievement, especially in reading and in other verbal skill areas, are common. Conduct Disorder is more frequent in boys than girls, with boys also exhibiting more aggressive behavior, while girls are more likely to engage in nonaggressive behaviors such as truancy, running away, and sexual misconduct.

Although many conduct-disordered adolescents settle down in their adult years and become reasonably stable, productive citizens, a substantial number continue to engage in antisocial behavior, including running afoul of the law.[9] Many, too, have poor interpersonal relationships and suffer from a variety of psychiatric problems, including alcoholism, drug abuse, and mood disorders. Those who are at greatest risk for problems in adult life are those who engage in more violent and aggressive kinds of behavior, especially at an early age; youngsters who confine their misbehavior to relatively minor infractions such as truancy and the like seem to have a better chance of "outgrowing" their difficulties. (We should note, however, that while running away falls into the "relatively minor" category youngsters who run away from home are at very high risk for physical and sexual abuse, substance abuse, prostitution, and even murder.) Conduct-disordered youngsters who come from broken homes or families in which there is a history of antisocial behavior, alcoholism, and aggression are also more likely than others to continue in a pattern of antisocial behavior as adults.[10]

Conduct Disorder is second to the anxiety disorders in terms of the frequency with which it co-occurs with mood disorders in young people.[11] Unlike the anxiety disorders, which typically occur in association with major depression, Conduct Disorder usually coexists with dysthymia.[12] It is considered to be a more serious complication because it is very difficult to treat and because it tends to persist into adult life, long after the mood disorder has resolved or responded to treatment.

OPPOSITIONAL DEFIANT DISORDER

Oppositional Defiant Disorder (ODD) is a relatively new diagnostic category, having first been described in 1980 in DSM III as "Oppositional Disorder." For a condition which affects so many children and which poses such pain and difficulty for parents, there has been surprisingly little research in the literature since then, so many questions still remain to be answered concerning the cause and most effective treatment for this disorder.

Children who are diagnosed with Oppositional Defiant Disorder are prone to negative, irritable moods and are frequently disobedient, defiant, and hostile toward authority figures. They are particularly likely to defy their parents, especially their mothers: although many are quite obedient and controlled with other adults, in the privacy of the home they are argumentative, provocative, unpredictable, and explosive. Their parents may aptly describe them as "always looking for trouble" because they often deliberately annoy others, goading both siblings and parents into screaming matches and physical altercations. These children are often unreasonably resentful of others and tend to be spiteful and vindictive, especially toward their siblings. They seem quite incapable of seeing how they engineer their own disasters and instead cast blame on others for any difficulties in which they find themselves.

The most baffling thing about these youngsters is the striking difference often seen between their behavior at home and their behavior in public settings, such as the classroom. As clinical psychologists, we have come away from more than one school conference about such children with the distinct impression that two entirely different children were discussed at the meeting: the well-behaved—even timid and submissive —child described by the teacher and the raging hell-terror that we and the parents knew the child could often be at home.

Since the symptoms of Oppositional Defiant Disorder are similar in nature to, but less severe than, those of Conduct Disorder—and since many youngsters with ODD go on to develop Conduct Disorder, some researchers consider ODD to be an early form of Conduct Disorder. Certainly, family histories of youngsters with ODD and CD have much in common: in both disorders, we frequently find families in which there are serious marital problems and in which at least one parent has a history of depression, Conduct Disorder, Attention-Deficit/Hyperactivity Disorder, and/or substance abuse.[13]

These findings, along with the fact that parents of ODD youngsters are often poor at providing supervision and consistent discipline, have led some researchers to suggest that ODD is caused by environmental factors. What these researchers cannot explain, however, is the fact that many ODD youngsters might be described as "spoiling for a fight" almost from the moment of birth: as infants, they have a generally negative temperament, including low frustration tolerance and quickness to anger. These researchers have also overlooked evidence from studies of adopted-away children showing that there is an hereditary factor in aggressive and antisocial behavior.[14]

ATTENTION-DEFICIT/HYPERACTIVITY DISORDER

Thanks to a great deal of scientific research, media publicity, and the unflagging efforts of parent-advocate groups, Attention-Deficit/Hyperactivity Disorder (ADHD) is certainly the childhood psychiatric disorder most widely recognized by the general public at this time. In fact, many youngsters who suffer from mood disorders are actually diagnosed not because a parent or teacher suspects depression but because someone believes that the child has symptoms of ADHD and brings the child to the attention of a mental health professional. (Often, the parent or teacher is at least partially correct, since about 20 to 30 percent of youngsters who are diagnosed with depression also have ADHD.)

To be diagnosed with ADHD, a child must have symptoms of either inattention or hyperactivity/impulsivity (see below and p. 36) which have persisted for at least six months. The symptoms must also be both maladaptive and inappropriate for the child's developmental level. Finally, the symptoms must be present before the age of seven years.

INATTENTION: Youngsters with this group of symptoms have difficulty sustaining attention, are easily distracted, and tend to avoid tasks which require sustained mental effort (e.g., schoolwork). They are prone to shift from one task or activity to another without seeing any through to completion. They are also frequently careless, messy, and disorganized in their work habits and notorious for chronic forgetfulness and for losing or misplacing their belongings.

Individuals with ADHD are said to have an "attentional bias toward novelty," because they seem to need more stimulation and variety than other children. Their problems with attention and concentration are particularly pronounced when they are faced with routine, monotonous activities, especially those which require close attention to detail. This is not to say that ADHD youngsters cannot sustain attention under any circumstances; in fact, when the activity is one of great interest to them, it may require herculean efforts to pull them away from it.

HYPERACTIVITY/IMPULSIVITY: Children with these problems are frequently described as "always on the go" or "acts like he's driven by a motor." They may talk excessively; have difficulty playing quietly; fidget and squirm; pop out of their seats when expected to remain seated; and climb or run about excessively when it is not appropriate to do so. Some children with ADHD are so energetic and hyperactive that they exhaust their parents and caretakers. Others manifest more subtle but still bothersome behaviors such as an inability to sit through meals without hopping up several times, talking incessantly, and making a variety of unusual noises during quiet activities.

Impulsivity in ADHD youngsters takes the form of impatience, difficulty delaying gratification ("I want it NOW!"), and a tendency to act before thinking about the consequences of their behavior. Parents and teachers describe such a child as one who constantly calls out in class, interrupts the conversation or play of others, and plunges into a task or activity before he has listened to the directions. Other children find him annoying because he must always be first in line, can't wait for his turn in activities, grabs toys and other objects from them, and can't abide by the rules of a game.

Most people with ADHD have symptoms of both inattention and hyperactivity/impulsivity. According to DSM IV, individuals with six or more symptoms in both areas should be diagnosed as Attention-Deficit/Hyperactivity Disorder, Combined Type, while those who have six or more symptoms of hyperactivity/impulsivity are categorized as ADHD, Predominantly Hyperactive Type.

Since not all individuals who merit a diagnosis of ADHD are excessively active or impulsive, DSM IV includes a third subtype of ADHD, known as Predominantly Inattentive Type. This is a sizable group of youngsters who have serious attentional problems but who are not hyperactive (some, in fact, actually appear underactive). Since their symptoms are less obvious and less troublesome to adults, these children were often overlooked in the past. We now know, however, that their problems—social, academic, and emotional—are as serious as those of the more classically hyperactive child.

We also know that ADHD children do not necessarily "outgrow" their difficulties. Although decreases in extremely high levels of activity may make the ADHD teenager less conspicuous in a group, only a minority of ADHD children— perhaps 20 percent or so—appear to be symptom-free by adolescence. Most continue to have problems with restlessness, inattentiveness, and impulsivity through the teen years and well into adult life.

What happens to these individuals in their adult years is still a matter of some controversy. On the one hand, noted researchers such as Dr. Russell Barkley at the University of Massachusetts report a poor adult outcome for many ADHD youngsters.[15] On the other hand, our own clinical experience indicates quite clearly that, as adults, many ADHD youngsters learn to compensate very well for their problems. Quite a few even turn their apparent liabilities into advantages: in professions such as emergency medicine, sales, and criminal law, a preference for novelty and excitement is a clear asset, as is a high level of energy. The difference between our findings and those of researchers such as Dr. Barkley probably reflects the fact that parents usually enter their children in research projects only after all else has failed. Thus, children who serve as research subjects are likely to be those whose symptoms are very severe.

LEARNING DISABILITIES

The term "learning disability" refers to a failure to learn despite an apparently normal capacity for learning. This means that not all children who perform poorly in school can be considered learning-disabled. For example, a child whose academic performance is deficient because he is blind or deaf is not considered learning-disabled, nor is the term used to refer to a child whose learning difficulties result from a generally low level of intelligence (mental retardation) or from severe environmental deprivation.

Federal guidelines state that, in order for a child to be considered learning-disabled, there must be a significant discrepancy between the child's potential for learning (as indicated by his scores on an intelligence test) and his actual academic achievement in one or more of seven areas. These include:

- Oral expression (speaking)

- Listening comprehension (understanding)

- Written expression

- Basic reading

- Reading comprehension

- Mathematics calculation

- Mathematics reasoning (problem solving)

Although researchers have used a variety of classification schemes to describe learning disabilities, for our purpose we can simply think of two broad classes of learning disabilities: (1) those which involve auditory-verbal processes, resulting in reading disorders and other language-based learning problems; and (2) those which involve visual and motor (nonverbal) processes, resulting in poor handwriting, difficulties in mathematics, and deficits in certain social skills.

Reading disorders, often referred to collectively as dyslexia, are by far the most common of the learning disabilities. Although some have suggested that reading disorders are caused by faulty eye movements or problems with visual perception, we now know that most reading-disabled individuals actually have problems with the way in which they process language, especially the relationship between sounds and symbols ("phonological processing").[16] Individuals with problems in this area also tend to have problems with spelling and writing, since both sets of skills depend on a solid grasp of sound-symbol relationships. Children with reading disorders often have a history of delayed speech and language development, problems pronouncing certain words and sounds, and difficulty finding the right words to express what they want to say.

The second group of learning disabilities—the nonverbal learning disabilities—occur much less frequently than language-based learning disabilities, accounting for only about 1–10 percent of children referred to learning-disability clinics. Children with nonverbal learning disabilities are deficient in their ability to recognize and organize visual patterns and to coordinate visual information with motor activity. They are often poorly coordinated in terms of both fine and gross motor skills, so they have difficulty learning to ride a bike, tie their shoes, and wield crayons and pencils. They have particular problems with handwriting, arithmetic, and nonverbal problem solving. Although they may have well-developed rote verbal memory, these youngsters have difficulty adapting to novel or complex situations. Because they are poor at perceiving nonverbal cues which are such an important component of communication, they often have significant problems with social skills and interpersonal relationships.

There is a clear link between learning disabilities and emotional problems, with some researchers reporting depressive symptoms in a third or more of the learning-disabled children they've studied.[17] Children with nonverbal learning disabilities seem to be particularly prone to depression and anxiety disorders. Dr. Byron Rourke, an authority on nonverbal learning disabilities, believes that a disturbance in the right hemisphere of the brain can account for both learning and emotional problems.[18]

THREE

Is My Child Depressed?

Diagnosing and Evaluating the Depressed Youngster

HOW DOES A DOCTOR MAKE THE DIAGNOSIS?

TO MANY PEOPLE, the way in which a psychologist or psychiatrist arrives at a diagnosis is baffling because it seems so different from what they are used to when they go to the family doctor with a physical complaint. When you take your child to the pediatrician for treatment of an earache or an upset stomach, you know that the doctor will begin by asking about the specific problem: where does it hurt? When did the pain begin? Has your child had a fever? A change in appetite? The doctor will also refer to your child's medical chart to refresh his memory concerning the child's general medical history.

Having obtained a history and a description of the problem, the physician proceeds to examine the youngster, often with the aid of instruments such as a stethoscope and an audioscope. On the basis of the history and his own observations, the doctor narrows down the possible diagnoses. To help confirm his diagnosis, he may order laboratory tests, such as blood tests or X rays. In fact, in our high-tech society, many people may even be suspicious of the doctor's diagnosis if he does not order such tests.

When a mental health professional is asked to diagnose a psychological problem, the methods used are quite different. However, the steps in the diagnostic process—history taking, examination, and testing—are the same.

TAKING A HISTORY: THE INITIAL INTERVIEW

Unlike the pediatrician, who has probably known your child for years and is, therefore, quite familiar with his medical and developmental history, a psychologist or psychiatrist must begin from scratch. Since psychological problems are often complex and can affect many aspects of a child's life, the mental health professional must gather a great deal of information about your child's general health and development, as well as information about his current level of functioning in all areas of life. You should be prepared to provide the following kinds of information.

- **Developmental history:** Was your child the product of a normal pregnancy, labor, and delivery or were there any complications? As a newborn, how did your child "settle in"? Did he meet age expectations for crawling, walking, talking, and toilet training, or were there delays in these areas?

- **Medical history:** Was your child generally healthy as an infant and toddler? Many depressed youngsters have a history of illness during the first year or so of life. Allergies, repeated ear infections and upper respiratory infections, surgeries, accidents, and hospitalizations should be noted, as well as any chronic medical conditions. Since depressed youngsters often complain of physical aches and pains, especially headaches and stomachaches, it is important to report these complaints.

- **Psychological history:** What has your child's general temperament been like? Would you describe him as laid back and easygoing or was he ornery and difficult from early days? Was he generally outgoing or was he rather shy and timid? Did he have severe temper tantrums? What about excessive separation anxiety: were there extreme problems separating from you to stay with a sitter or go to nursery school? Pronounced fears and phobias should also be reported: youngsters at risk for mood and anxiety disorders often have a history of strong negative reactions to such common childhood experiences as Halloween costumes and circus clowns.

- **Educational history:** Depressed youngsters often have a history of poor or erratic performance in school. Many also have coexisting learning disabilities or attentional problems which further contribute to academic problems. If you have saved your child's report cards, take copies of them to the interview and, if your child has had educational testing or a speech/language evaluation, take a copy of the report with you, as well as reports from tutors or other educational specialists who have been involved with the youngster.

- **Family history:** Your doctor isn't just being snoopy when he or she asks rather personal questions about your relationship with your spouse, since family discord can have a profound effect on a child's emotional state. Other questions you should be prepared to answer frankly concern mood and anxiety disorders, alcoholism, and learning disabilities in blood relatives going back to your grandparents.

To help you organize information beforehand, the doctor may ask you to complete a number of different questionnaires and bring them with you to the first appointment or return them by mail. A typical history questionnaire is provided in Appendix A.

Who should attend the initial interview? Some mental health professionals, especially those trained specifically in family therapy, insist on seeing the entire family at the initial interview. We think, however, that parents should meet alone with the mental health professional on the first visit. This allows you to determine whether you are comfortable with the professional and whether you think your child will be comfortable as well. An initial meeting with the professional also puts you in a better position to prepare your child for a meeting.

Separate interviews with parent and child also protect the privacy and confidentiality of both parents and youngster. Parents may be reluctant, for example, to talk openly about personal or marital problems in front of the child, while the child, in turn, may hesitate to reveal his feelings in the presence of his parents. Sensitive parents, too, are appropriately worried that reciting a "laundry list" of complaints about an already demoralized child in his presence will only compound the child's poor self-esteem. Often, if the youngster is present when his parents describe their concerns, the child becomes defensive, arguing and debating every point. The result is, at best, confusion and, at worst, open warfare—certainly not a great way to begin!

EXPLORING THE PROBLEM: INTERVIEW WITH THE CHILD

Very few teenagers and virtually no younger children seek mental health services of their own accord. Many, in fact, actively resist the notion that they are in need of help. This is especially true of teenagers, in whom shame and embarrassment may take the form of denial ("I don't have any problems:

my parents are the problem"), withdrawal, and even overt hostility toward the mental health professional. In our clinical experience, resistant youngsters are usually much more cooperative when interviewed alone than when parents are included: the presence of two or more adults during the interview can make some young people feel threatened and defensive. Also, as we noted above, children may be more apt to disclose information about painful thoughts, feelings, and experiences if they are assured of confidentiality.*

Experienced mental health professionals are not surprised when an interview with a child yields very different information from that provided by the parents. In general, children tend to underreport behavior and conduct problems such as school problems, aggression, and disobedience. As one noted expert points out, this doesn't mean that the child is deliberately lying: he simply may not be particularly bothered by symptoms that his parents find very irksome.[1] Parents, on the other hand, are frequently unaware of emotional symptoms such as decreased energy, anxiety, obsessions, self-dislike, and suicidal ideas, so they tend to underreport in these areas.

> *At age fifteen Meredith had a long history of academic difficulties. The adopted daughter of well-to-do parents, she had been tested by a virtual army of experts and had received private tutoring since second grade, with no appreciable improvement. It was a tutor working on his degree in school psychology who finally recognized Meredith's problems with attention and recommended that she be evaluated for Attention-Deficit Disorder.*
>
> *Meredith's mother scheduled an appointment for an evaluation and immediately began to read up on Attention-Deficit Disorder. She was able to provide the child*

---

* With children and adolescents, confidentiality means that no information provided by the youngster will be revealed to the parents without the youngster's permission unless his behavior poses a danger to himself or others (e.g., suicide or homicide).

psychiatrist with a great deal of information about her daughter's development, as well as report cards and evaluation results dating back to Meredith's earliest school experiences. She described her daughter as a sensible, mature youngster who had an agreeable, easygoing disposition but who had always had difficulty with attention and concentration. By the end of the initial interview, Meredith's mother, at least, was convinced that the source of Meredith's problems had at last been diagnosed. "I can't wait to have you see Meredith," she said. "I feel like we've really hit the nail on the head."

When Meredith herself was interviewed, however, a very different picture emerged. Although she readily acknowledged problems with concentration, especially when schoolwork was involved, she dismissed these difficulties as minor in comparison with repeated episodes of depression. She described problems with sleep, appetite, and very low mood, noting: "It was really bad in seventh grade. I was so miserable that I really wanted to die. In fact, I actually started taking pills from my parents' medicine cabinet and stashing them in a hiding place. I probably would have gone through with it—killed myself, I mean—if my grandparents hadn't come to visit and taken me back to Michigan to spend the summer with them."

Of course, before an interview can yield any kind of information, the child must actually attend the interview. What if your child is so angry or so defensive that he threatens to boycott the appointment? What if he says, "Okay, you can make me go but you can't make me talk"? Certainly, if a youngster is so out of control that parental authority is not enough to bring him to the appointment, the situation is grave. In such cases we usually suggest that the parents establish an alliance with a professional who can help them set and enforce limits with the young person.

Much of the time, however, we find that even the most

difficult and rebellious of youngsters can be convinced to attend at least an initial appointment if they are informed that their input is important. The purpose of the evaluation, it should be explained, is not just to find out what is "wrong" with the youngster but to try to figure out how things can be changed for the better at home, in school, with friends, and so on. In many cases, if the interview goes well, the young person opens up and becomes much more willing to discuss his perception of the problem.

DIAGNOSTIC TESTS, SELF-REPORT MEASURES, AND RATING SCALES

MEDICAL LABORATORY TESTS. It comes as a great surprise to many parents to learn that there are no blood tests or other clinical laboratory measures currently available to detect depression. Scientists have avidly pursued the development of such lab tests, but with mixed results so far.

One such diagnostic test, for example, known as the dexamethasone suppression test (DST), was initially hailed with enthusiasm as a surefire means of detecting depression. Subsequent research, however, has shown that the DST cannot be used with confidence as a diagnostic test since it correctly identifies only about 45 to 50 percent of depressed adults and incorrectly identifies about 20 percent of schizophrenic patients and about 7 percent of normal controls as suffering from depression.[2] Results of this test in depressed children and adolescents are even less reliable than those obtained with adults.[3]

The attempt to use the DST as a diagnostic test for depression had its origin in the fact that, during an episode of depression, about 50 percent of depressed adults have elevated levels of cortisol, a hormone secreted by the adrenal gland. Aberrations in the way in which depressed patients secrete other hormones such as growth hormone and thyroid hormones* have also been found and they, too, have raised hopes that we might find reliable biological "markers" for depression. Here too, however, results have been generally disappointing.

Researchers have also studied disruption in biological rhythms in depression by monitoring sleep patterns. In depressed adults, recording of brain electrical activity during sleep (polysomnography) has revealed differences in sleep patterns, including more eye movements during the rapid eye movement (REM) phase of sleep associated with dreaming and later onset of REM sleep. Although clinicians who work with depressed children and adolescents can attest to the frequency of insomnia, nightmares, and altered sleep cycles in their patients, researchers have not yet identified consistent differences in sleep patterns in this population.[4]

A somewhat more promising approach to identifying a specific marker for depression in children and adolescents involves measuring changes in motor activity across the course of a day. Using a small device attached to the child's belt, researchers at Harvard Medical School monitored patterns of motor activity in depressed and nondepressed youngsters and found that the patterns differed markedly between the two groups.[5] This approach needs to be studied with larger groups of children and adolescents before we will know if it can serve as a practical aid in the diagnosis of mood disorders in this population.

Finally, we should note that an exciting new area of child psychiatry research involves the application of brain imaging techniques, such as computerized tomography and magnetic resonance imaging, to the study of brain structure and function in depression and other psychiatric conditions. These

---

* The findings of endocrine abnormalities associated with depression should not be taken to mean that these abnormalities cause depression, nor should we assume that depression can be treated by correcting these abnormalities (e.g., through use of thyroid medication).

techniques certainly appear to hold promise for the future but at the present time they are primarily research techniques which are not suitable for clinical use.

PHYSICAL EXAMINATION. While there are no laboratory tests to identify depression, children in whom depression is suspected will need to undergo a physical examination, as well as blood tests, urinalysis, and an electrocardiogram (EKG). These tests can help rule out a physical cause of symptoms, such as thyroid problems or the existence of a tumor. They are also necessary to provide the child psychiatrist with a baseline against which any changes which might be associated with medication can be assessed.

A physical examination is not needed to make a diagnosis of depression. However, most depressed youngsters will have had such an examination prior to seeing a mental health professional since parents usually turn first to their pediatrician when children have emotional or behavioral problems. (In fact, since depressed youngsters are prone to all sorts of physical complaints and illnesses, it is often the case that the youngster will have seen the pediatrician on numerous occasions in the recent past.)

When assessing a child in whom depression is suspected, many pediatricians include neurological screening as part of the physical examination. This is done to rule out the possibility of a disease of the central nervous system. In the very unlikely event that such a problem were detected, the pediatrician would refer the child to a neurologist for further evaluation. Unless the pediatrician suspects that your child suffers from a seizure disorder (epilepsy), there is no reason for the child to have an electroencephalogram (EEG: a test of electrical activity in the brain, used to diagnose epilepsy).

PSYCHOLOGICAL TESTS. Psychological tests can be broadly divided into two categories: (1) performance tests; and (2) symptom and personality measures. **Performance tests** include tests of intellectual functioning (IQ tests) and achievement tests, designed to assess academic achievement. Among the most widely used tests are the Wechsler Intelligence Scale for Children (WISC III), the Wide Range Achievement Test (WRAT), the Peabody Individual Achievement Test (PIAT), and the Woodcock-Johnson Psychoeducational Battery.

Although these tests are not helpful in terms of making a diagnosis of depression, they are essential if your child has a history of poor school performance or if there are concerns about the child's ability to reason, judge, and make decisions at a level appropriate for his age. These tests also afford the evaluator the opportunity to observe the manner in which your child faces intellectually and academically challenging tasks. The child's comments during testing can also offer a window into his feelings of competence and self-esteem.

If your child has a history of attentional problems in addition to depression, the doctor may also administer performance tests designed to assess attention span and impulsivity. Three such tests are the Gordon Diagnostic System,[6] the Test of Variables of Attention,[7] and the Continuous Performance Test.[8] While these performance tests are not infallible, they can provide the doctor with useful information about a youngster's ability to keep his attention focused on a task and refrain from responding in an impulsive manner.

Symptom and personality measures include questionnaires and inventories, usually in true-false or multiple choice format, and so-called "projective tests," such as the Rorschach Inkblot Technique. Projective tests have no "right" or "wrong" answers. Instead, the youngster must use his imagination to see shapes in the inkblots or, in the case of the Thematic Apperception Test, to make up stories about pictures he is shown. The child's responses and stories are believed to reveal his own inner needs, fears, and struggles. Whether or not this approach to personality assessment yields useful information has been the subject of debate among professionals for many years. Projective tests are time-consuming and expensive and, since we believe that they do not yield any more information than can be obtained in a clinical interview, we do not recommend them as a primary means of diagnosing psychiatric disorders, including depression.

On the other hand, questionnaires and rating scales can provide a great deal of useful information about how the child functions in different settings and about how he sees himself. Sometimes, in fact, a youngster who gives bland, noncommittal replies in an interview will actually reveal much more about his true feelings when he responds to a structured questionnaire, such as the Children's Depression Inventory.[9] This twenty-seven-item questionnaire, developed by Dr. Maria Kovacs at the University of Pittsburgh, taps a variety of areas which are often problematic for depressed youngsters, including self-concept, physical complaints, social problems, and depressed mood. Sample items from this scale are presented in Chart 3.1.

The Reynolds Adolescent Depression Scale[10] is a similar scale designed for use with adolescents. Sample items from this scale are presented in Chart 3.2.

Other useful self-report measures include the Revised Children's Manifest Anxiety Scale (see Chart 3.3), the Minnesota Multiphasic Personality Inventory, and the Millon Adolescent Personality Inventory. Questionnaires like these do double duty, since they allow comparison of the child's score with that obtained by other children, and they also provide the mental health professional with clues about specific problem areas as the child experiences them.

Finally, rating scales completed by parents and other people in the child's natural environment can provide important information about how the child behaves across a variety of settings. For example, mental health professionals often ask parents to complete rating scales like the Child Behavior Checklist or the Behavioral Screening Questionnaire, both of which assess a wide range of emotional and behavioral symptoms. Although there are several rating scales which help us collect useful information about children who suffer from other conditions, such as Attention-Deficit/Hyperactivity Dis-

CHART 3.1
CHILDREN'S DEPRESSION INVENTORY

1. _____ I AM SAD ONCE IN A WHILE
   _____ I AM SAD MANY TIMES
   _____ I AM SAD ALL THE TIME

2. _____ NOTHING WILL EVER WORK OUT FOR ME
   _____ I AM NOT SURE IF THINGS WILL WORK OUT
   FOR ME
   _____ THINGS WILL WORK OUT FOR ME OK

3. _____ I DO MOST THINGS OK
   _____ I DO MANY THINGS WRONG
   _____ I DO EVERYTHING WRONG

4. _____ I HAVE FUN IN MANY THINGS
   _____ I HAVE FUN IN SOME THINGS
   _____ NOTHING IS FUN AT ALL

The Children's Depression Inventory was developed by Maria Kovacs, Ph.D. This portion of it is reprinted with the permission of the publisher: Multi-Health Systems, Inc., 908 Niagara Falls Blvd., N. Tonawanda, NY 14120-2060, 1-800-456-3003.

CHART 3.2
REYNOLDS ADOLESCENT
DEPRESSION SCALE

(Sample Form)

	Almost Never	Hardly Ever	Some Times	Most of the Time
1. I feel happy	☐	☐	☐	☐
2. I worry about school	☐	☐	☐	☐
3. I feel lonely	☐	☐	☐	☐
4. I feel my parents don't like me	☐	☐	☐	☐
5. I feel important	☐	☐	☐	☐
6. I feel like hiding from people	☐	☐	☐	☐
7. I feel sad	☐	☐	☐	☐
8. I feel like crying	☐	☐	☐	☐
9. I feel that no one cares about me	☐	☐	☐	☐
10. I feel like having fun with other students	☐	☐	☐	☐

The Reynolds Adolescent Depression Scale was developed by William Reynolds, Ph.D. Sample items are reprinted by permission of the publisher: Psychological Assessment Resources, Inc.

Chart 3.3
REVISED CHILDREN'S MANIFEST ANXIETY SCALE

1. I have trouble making up my mind. <u>YES</u> <u>NO</u>

2. I get nervous when things do not go the right way for me. <u>YES</u> <u>NO</u>

3. Others seem to do things easier than I can. <u>YES</u> <u>NO</u>

4. I like everyone I know. <u>YES</u> <u>NO</u>

5. Often I have trouble getting my breath. <u>YES</u> <u>NO</u>

6. I worry a lot of the time. <u>YES</u> <u>NO</u>

7. I am afraid of a lot of things. <u>YES</u> <u>NO</u>

8. I am always kind. <u>YES</u> <u>NO</u>

9. I get mad easily. <u>YES</u> <u>NO</u>

10. I worry about what my parents will say to me. <u>YES</u> <u>NO</u>

The *Revised Children's Manifest Anxiety Scale* was developed by Cecil Reynold, Ph.D., and Bert Richmond, Ed.D. Sample items reprinted by permission of the publisher, Western Psychological Services, 12031 Wilshire Boulevard, Los Angeles, CA 90025.

order, rating scales specifically designed for assessing the behavior of depressed children are still in the process of development. (One such scale, the Depression Symptom Checklist, currently being tested by the authors, is reproduced in Appendix D.)

Researchers have consistently found that teachers are often unaware of the extent to which a youngster suffers from depression, since most depressed youngsters manage to "hold it together" in school and rarely act out in ways that would attract a teacher's attention. However, teachers are often sensitive to subtle signs of depression, such as poor schoolwork or social isolation. They are also an invaluable source of other kinds of information about children: since, for example, there is often reason to suspect coexisting Attention-Deficit/Hyperactivity Disorder or learning disabilities, teacher input is an essential component of the diagnostic process.

ASSOCIATED CONDITIONS

When a mental health professional evaluates a youngster in whom depression is suspected, he must also consider alternative diagnoses which could explain the symptoms he sees. In this, he is similar to a pediatrician who must decide whether a child's red, itchy rash is caused by measles, chicken pox, an encounter with poison ivy, or something else altogether.

As we discussed in Chapter 2, many youngsters who suffer from depressive disorders also suffer simultaneously from other psychiatric disorders. This means that the task of the child psychiatrist or psychologist is in some ways more complicated than that of the pediatrician: even when depression has been correctly identified and diagnosed, the doctor must still look for ("rule out") other conditions which often accompany the identified disorder—conditions such as anxiety disorders, Conduct Disorder, or learning disabilities.

As clinical psychologists, we often encounter youngsters who have had all sorts of evaluations by all sorts of specialists but who have never undergone an assessment focusing on what we might call "the big picture." If, for example, a depressed youngster with learning and attentional problems is evaluated by a learning-disabilities specialist, the diagnosis of learning disabilities will be made. However, the recommended tutoring and classroom accommodations will be of no avail unless the attentional and emotional problems are also addressed. Conversely, if only the attentional and emotional problems are identified, treatment results will be poor as the youngster continues to flounder in school.

Nelson had good reason to be, as he put it, "fed up with doctors and all their stupid tests and questions." At age ten and in the fifth grade, he had had numerous evaluations over the years as his parents had sought with increasing desperation to identify the cause of his poor self-esteem, irritable mood, social difficulties, and academic struggles.

In preschool, his problems with concentration and following directions were thought to be linked to his delayed motor skills, so he received an occupational therapy evaluation and went through a course of sensory integrative therapy. In first grade, he had difficulty learning to read, so a learning-disability evaluation was obtained and a tutor was employed to help him in second grade. By third grade, while schoolwork continued poor, temper outbursts had become commonplace and Nelson was increasingly ostracized by his classmates and neighborhood children. A psychologist did not address attentional or learning problems but did diagnose depression. He worked with Nelson in individual psychotherapy for a year until Nelson's fourth-grade teacher suggested that Nelson be evaluated for Attention-Deficit/Hyperactivity Disorder. His parents dutifully obtained a consultation from a neurologist who overlooked the depression but diagnosed ADHD and prescribed treatment with stimu-

lant medication. Medication was continued over the course of the year, in spite of the fact that Nelson complained of side effects and seemed rather "druggy" on the medication.

When, in fifth grade, Nelson was seen by yet another professional, he was a thoroughly demoralized youngster who had little reason to believe that doctors could offer real help with his problems. His parents, too, were worn out from their efforts and quite dubious about putting their child through any more tests or diagnostic procedures.

This professional, however, spent a great deal of time poring over the records and reports of the other professionals who had worked with Nelson. With their observations and findings in mind, he interviewed Nelson and his parents and concluded that each of his predecessors had been at least partially correct: Nelson did indeed suffer from depression, attentional problems, and learning disabilities. Only when all of the pieces were considered together, however, was it possible to devise a treatment plan that would truly be of help to Nelson.

In summary, the entire diagnostic process is admittedly complex. There are no "foolproof" diagnostic tests, the situation is often complicated by the presence of coexisting disorders, and the process can be quite expensive and time-consuming. However, unless all of the child's needs are identified, an effective treatment plan cannot be implemented.

OBTAINING AN EVALUATION

As a parent, how do you go about finding a psychologist or psychiatrist who is skilled in evaluating and diagnosing the problems of depressed children? When it comes to choosing a mental health professional to work with your child, you want to apply a more thoughtful strategy than simply flipping through the Yellow Pages. Where can you turn for help?

Your friends, neighbors, and colleagues are probably among the best sources of information. If a close friend with whom you have much in common tells you that Dr. X was helpful to her child and her family, it is likely that you, too, will find Dr. X to be of help.

If your friends and family cannot provide you with the names of some competent mental health professionals, your next step should be a consultation with your child's pediatrician or family practice doctor. Other good referral sources include the guidance counselor, principal, or school psychologist at your child's school.

COPING WITH A DIAGNOSIS OF DEPRESSION

When, after careful evaluation, a credible professional tells you, "Your child is suffering from depression," you are likely to experience a flood of conflicting emotions. One parent of a depressed child described her reaction this way:

"How did I feel when the doctor told me my daughter was depressed? Even though I'd suspected it all along, my first reaction was still a scared, sinking feeling and I wanted to scream, "Oh, no, not my daughter." I guess I really wanted to believe that there was nothing wrong with Cindy—that she could control her behavior and her moods if she really wanted to. Maybe that was less frightening than the idea of something that neither one of us could control.

"My husband took it even harder than I did. At first, he just wouldn't accept it. He was angry with the doctor, as if it were somehow the doctor's fault. All along, he had said that Cindy was just spoiled and that if we—meaning me—cracked down on her, she'd shape up. Now here was

this doctor telling us that it wasn't me, it wasn't us: something really was wrong with our daughter.

"I think that one of the reasons that it hit my husband so hard is because there's a lot of depression on his side of the family. One of his uncles committed suicide and his mother has been in and out of hospitals for years. I know that he's afraid that Cindy will have to go through the same things. I think he feels guilty, too, like it's his fault for passing this on to our daughter."

Most parents of depressed youngsters experience at least some of the feelings described above. Young people, too, may react with strong feelings, especially to recommendations for therapy and medication. Many youngsters are greatly relieved when a name is finally given to their problem and express eagerness to begin treatment immediately. Others, however, stoutly deny the existence of difficulties and refuse to cooperate with the proposed treatment, medical or psychological.

Thirteen-year-old Will was a gifted youngster who breezed through the early years of elementary school. In fourth grade, however, he witnessed the accidental drowning of a friend and subsequently developed nightmares and a variety of fears and phobias. He became increasingly fearful of being alone and of leaving the house and, within a short time, he was adamant in his refusal to attend school.

Will responded very well to a combined program of medication and psychotherapy and soon returned to school, where he performed reasonably well academically and rejoined his friends in extracurricular activities. His mood, however, never really returned to pretrauma levels. He wasn't a behavior problem in school but he was often irritable and argumentative at home and prone to fly into a rage when his parents corrected him or set limits on his behavior.

During a particularly severe outburst, Will put his

fist through a window and required emergency-room treatment for his injuries. Shaken, his parents obtained a consultation with a psychologist who found that, while Will had made great progress, he had never fully recovered from his earlier trauma and had developed dysthymia. He recommended that Will resume psychotherapy with his former therapist and that he also be evaluated by a psychiatrist who could prescribe appropriate medication.

Although Will listened with apparent interest as the psychologist explained his findings, he quietly but adamantly refused to consider another trial of medication. "There's nothing wrong with me," he explained. "Okay, so I lose my temper once in a while: you would, too, if you had to live with my parents. But I'm not crazy and I'm not going to take any more pills!"

After considerable discussion, Will did agree to resume treatment with his former therapist. With the help of his therapist, he eventually decided to undergo another trial of medication which ultimately proved beneficial to him.

What can you do if your child rejects the diagnosis, the proposed treatment, or both? With younger children, this problem seldom arises, although some very irritable, hyper-aroused youngsters may routinely put up a fuss about taking medication or attending therapy sessions. With a resistant teenager, however, the situation is obviously much more complicated. Certainly, you can't physically drag an unwilling teenager into the therapist's office, nor can you hold him down and force him to swallow medication. What are your options?

We think that the wisest course of action is to convey quietly but firmly that the situation is not open to negotiation: the decision will be made by you, the parents—not by the child. Just as with a toddler who angrily protests at not being allowed to play in traffic, the message is a simple one: "My job as a parent is to make decisions which serve to protect you, even if you don't like the decisions." Thus the decision to participate in treatment is not the child's—it is yours, as a parent.* This does not mean that you will haul the child, kicking and screaming, into the doctor's office or force-feed medications. It does mean, however, that you will take responsibility for seeing that your child's need for appropriate treatment is met. Especially with teenagers, you can make access to a variety of desirable activities, such as driving the car, contingent on the youngster's participation in treatment. While this "barter system" may not be good on a long-term basis, it often serves to engage the resistant adolescent in the treatment process.

Sometimes it is not the child but one parent who disagrees with the diagnosis and/or the recommendations for treatment. What can you do if you, as a parent, are faced with this situation? You can, of course, agree to obtain a second opinion from another mental health professional. In our clinical experience, however, such marked disagreement is usually a signal of more extensive marital discord—a signal that parents are so much at odds with each other that they cannot come together to agree on something as important as their child's emotional functioning and well-being. There are no firm rules to follow in a situation like this, but if you are the parent who wants to pursue treatment we urge you to persevere in your efforts to obtain the best treatment for your child. Sometimes, unfortunately, this can require a court to intervene in the best interests of the child.

Finally, it is important to realize that the purpose of a diagnostic evaluation is not simply to attach a diagnostic label

---

* With resistant adolescents, individual therapy is often preferable to family therapy, since the latter is apt to be more threatening to the youngster, forcing him into a "macho" position from which he cannot easily retreat. If the youngster can form a relationship in individual therapy, his therapist can help him accept the need for adjunctive family work and/or medication, as needed.

as a means of "explaining" the child's problems. No matter how thorough and painstaking the evaluation, neither you nor your child will be well served if you do not understand the implications of the diagnosis, the way in which it was made, and the recommendations that stem from it. Don't leave your common sense outside the office door! If you don't understand something—a term, a procedure, the reason for a specific recommendation—speak up! The professional is there to answer your questions and to assist you in obtaining the most effective and efficient treatment for your child.

FOUR

What Causes Depression?

IF YOUR CHILD is diagnosed as suffering from depression, your first question is likely to be "What went wrong?" Most commonly, parents assume that the fault lies with them; that something they did (or something they failed to do) caused the problem. Parents are particularly likely to assume that they are to blame or to blame each other if there has been a divorce or if, as is often the case, one parent suffers from depression, alcoholism, or another psychiatric disorder.

ARE PARENTS TO BLAME?

If you are the parent of a depressed youngster, you don't have to be told that some of the people you hold nearest and dearest are quite ready to lay the blame for your child's problems at your feet. Total strangers—people in the grocery store or on the street—may chime in, especially if the depressed youngster also suffers from Oppositional Defiant Disorder or Conduct Disorder, because these children often appear "bratty" and "spoiled" to other adults.

PARENT BASHING

Even mental health professionals, people from whom a beleaguered parent should certainly expect empathy and support, may join in what has been called "parent bashing," suggesting in subtle or not so subtle ways that parents have in some way caused the problem. In fact, the notion that parental behavior determines child adjustment has received strong support from child psychiatrists and child psychologists over the years. Mental health professionals trained in the Freudian approach often minimize the role of biological factors and emphasize the importance of early life experiences in determining personality and psychological adjustment. According to this school of thought, a child's relationship with his parents is foremost among these early life experiences. For years, many professionals thought that cold, rejecting parents ("refrigerator parents") actually caused the incapacitating neurological condition called autism. Other psychologists and psychiatrists described "schizophrenogenic mothers" as a major factor in the development of schizophrenia, a serious progressive mental disorder. Some even advocated "parentectomy," a tongue-in-cheek way of saying, "Get this kid away from his parents and he'll be okay."

> *"I'm not sure you can help me—probably you're going to tell me it's all my fault. But I just had to try one more time." The grave-faced woman in the psychiatrist's office handed over the file on her eight-year-old son as she spoke. "It's all in there," she said. "When Brandon was three years old and throwing the world's worst tantrums, I took him to Dr. X, who told me that my marital problems were causing Brandon's problems. Two years later,*

*after my husband and I were divorced, I saw Dr. Y, who
said that Brandon's problems were due to the divorce.
Last year I went to Dr. Z. He said that I'm a very needy,
controlling mother and that, if I could just let Brandon be
his own person, everything would be fine."*

*She paused for a moment, then added, "Look, Doc-
tor, maybe it is me. Maybe I am the cause of all of Brandon's problems. I don't know. I just know I've done the
best I can do and nothing seems to work."*

The media and the popular press have contributed to parent bashing too. Books with titles like *Toxic Parents*[1] have
furthered the belief that otherwise normal youngsters are
driven into mental illness by the behavior of malignant parents. And does a week pass when Oprah or Phil Donahue
doesn't feature an interview with people who blame their poor
adjustment as adults on the injustices done to them as children?

What do we really know? What evidence is there that
poor parenting causes depression in young people?

FAMILY DYSFUNCTION AND CHILDHOOD DEPRESSION

Certainly depressed youngsters' perceptions of their families
are more negative than those of other youngsters and, the
more depressed the young person, the more negative are his
perceptions of the way in which his family functions.[2] Specifically, depressed children and adolescents describe their parents as distant, unsupportive, and emotionally unavailable.
These youngsters report frequent conflicts with their parents—
conflicts which are often highly emotionally charged. They see
their parents as intolerant and inflexible and they feel that they
themselves are allowed little say in decision making within the
family. Finally, depressed youngsters report that their families
are seldom involved, as families, in social, religious, or recreational activities.[3]

Since depression distorts the way in which a person views the world, before we can accept these perceptions we must check on their accuracy. In other words, we must ask whether other family members see the family in the same light. For the most part, the answer is "Yes." When parents of depressed children are asked to describe family relations, they also describe parent-child relationships which are cold, hostile, and tense. They also describe relationships in which there is little sharing of thoughts, feelings, or recreational activities. Compared with parents of nondepressed children, parents of depressed children are more authoritarian and controlling ("Do it because I said so!") in their interactions with their children. They also use physical punishment more frequently than parents whose children are not depressed.[4]

We find, too, that parents who are themselves depressed (and that includes many parents of depressed youngsters) seem to have specific parenting problems. For example, researchers have found that, since high levels of irritability often accompany depression, depressed parents are likely to be slow to praise but very quick to criticize, nag, and scold.[5] They are also less likely to use explanations, reasoning, and persuasion in managing their children.[6] Finally, depressed parents may also have impaired problem-solving and coping skills, so their parenting may be impaired in other ways as well.

After observing these patterns, many mental health professionals have concluded that parents are to blame for the depressed child's difficulties. The child's depression, they reason, is simply a predictable response to poor parenting and growing up in a difficult, stressful environment. Some have suggested that children who are exposed to years of negative, unpredictable, and capricious parental behavior develop a pattern of "learned helplessness"; that is, they come to view events in their lives as uncontrollable and beyond their ability to manage.[7] Others have speculated that, just as they learn other things through imitation, children actually learn depressed patterns of thinking and behaving by imitating a parent who is depressed.

There are, however, some serious flaws with the theory that depression in children and adolescents is caused by poor parenting. For example, if poor parenting causes depression, why are the child's problems sometimes apparent from the earliest days of life? How can we explain why so many depressed children have a history of health problems in infancy[8] or why they have such a high incidence of neurological "soft signs" (minor abnormalities in motor, sensory, and integrative function, such as poor fine motor coordination, poor balance, and irregular, jerky movements)?[9]* It is unlikely that these problems have anything to do with poor parenting. Nor can this theory account for the fact that many parents of depressed children have successfully raised other children who seem to be quite well adjusted and who have no symptoms of depression or other psychiatric disorders.

Finally, the blame-the-parents hypothesis is based on the assumption that influence flows in one direction only—from parent to child—and that child behavior has no effect on parent reactions. This assumption is both simplistic and incorrect, as we shall explain in the following section.

THE CHILD'S CONTRIBUTION

If children were simply "blank slates" at birth, blaming parents for the way in which children develop would make sense. But the reality is that children are not just blank slates upon which experience writes.

Parents have always known what research has only recently revealed: babies are born with individual personal

---

* Scientists believe that motor soft signs reflect disorders in a region of the brain known as the basal ganglia. Research has demonstrated that dysfunction in the basal ganglia is also associated with emotional disorders such as depression and Obsessive Compulsive Disorder.

styles, or **temperaments,** which are obvious from the first hours of life and are surprisingly stable across time. Some infants are adaptable and easygoing right from the start. They seem to take things in stride and can tolerate new experiences and changes in schedule with a minimum of fuss. If they're wet or hungry, they make their needs known with whimpers or quiet cries and, once their needs have been met, they settle quickly into contentment. Other infants are much more vigorous and intense in their responses. If their needs are not met immediately—if a feeding is delayed, for example—they burst into earsplitting screams and they take much longer to calm down after the problem has been remedied. In a similar vein, some babies quickly settle into a predictable pattern of eating, sleeping, and eliminating while others are very irregular in their habits and never seem to develop regular routines.

In a fascinating investigation that followed a large group of children from birth through late adolescence, psychologists Stella Chess and Alexander Thomas identified nine basic elements of temperament, including activity level, adaptability, intensity of reaction, and positive or negative mood.[10] On the basis of their research, they were able to identify temperamental styles which were apparent from birth and fairly stable across time. Although styles can overlap in some children, for our purposes we can focus on three major temperamental styles:

- **Easy children** accounted for about 40 percent of the children in the study group. Easy children are generally positive in mood, adjust well to change, and quickly adapt to schedules and routines. They are slow to anger, low-key in the intensity of their reactions, and easy to soothe and comfort.

- **Slow-to-warm-up children** don't like change. They have difficulty dealing with new situations and typically react to new foods, new people, and new settings with anxiety and withdrawal. If they are suddenly thrust into a new situation, they may protest vigorously but, if allowed to proceed at their own pace, they usually make a good adjustment.

- **Difficult children** are just that—difficult! These youngsters, who made up about 10 percent of the original study group, have difficulty settling into a predictable routine. They are overly sensitive, easily irritated, and hard to soothe. Their mood is generally negative and they react poorly to new situations. They are intense and forceful in their reactions and they have problems letting go of a bad mood.

TEMPERAMENT AND PSYCHOLOGICAL PROBLEMS. Over the long haul, what happens to babies who are "difficult" or "slow to warm up"? Do they fare differently, as a group, from youngsters who are characterized as having an "easy" temperament? In many cases, we find that temperament in infancy does have long-term implications for psychological adjustment in later life. While an easy temperament is not a passport to good adult adjustment and a difficult temperament certainly does not preordain a later diagnosis of psychiatric problems, children with extremely difficult temperaments are represented in disproportionate numbers among those who come to the attention of mental health professionals.[11]

Several researchers have found, for example, that marked shyness and social withdrawal in early childhood may portend later problems with fears, loneliness, and depression.[12] Concerning mood disorders, in particular, a connection has also been observed between a tendency to become easily and intensely upset ("emotionality") in infancy and early childhood and increased risk for major depression in later childhood and adolescence.[13] This has led some researchers to speculate that difficult temperament reflects problems in the same neuroendocrine systems that have been implicated in depression (see p. 76). It may also be the case that the child's difficult temperament brings him into frequent conflict with his parents, interfering with the development of a healthy parent-child relationship and leaving the child vulnerable to depression.

TEMPERAMENT AND PARENT-CHILD INTERACTION. We know that difficult temperament can have an impact on the relationship between a child and his parents right from the start. Parents who have coped with difficult youngsters can testify that such children can drive even the most patient of parents to despair. Many say that they quickly learned to treat their difficult child differently from their other children because his behavior demanded a different approach.

"We never have bedtime problems with Sean or Kerry; a story, a good night kiss, turn out the lights, and that's it until morning. With Brendan, it's a different story. He fights going to bed and, if one of us doesn't lie down with him until he falls asleep, he cries and carries on so much that the other two can't sleep. Even after he finally falls asleep, it usually isn't long before he's in our room, begging to sleep with us. Sometimes we're just too tired to fight with him, so we give in and let him sleep on the floor in our room."

"Alexis is so moody and irritable. It's like living with a time bomb: you never know what's going to set her off. The other kids complain that we let her get away with all kinds of horrible behavior—things we'd never let them get away with. The sad part is that they're right; we all walk on eggs around her."

We can see, then, that the behavior of a temperamentally difficult child can exert a great deal of influence on the tenor of the child's relationship with his parents.* In similar fashion, the behavior of a depressed youngster can also affect the par-

---

* Once again, the influence is not in one direction only. When there is a poor "fit" between the child's temperament and that of the parent—when, for example, a vivacious, energetic mother is paired with a placid, retiring baby (or vice versa)—

ent-child relationship. There is evidence from the work of pioneering researcher Dr. Joaquim Puig-Antich that the irritability, social withdrawal, and low mood of the depressed child directly contribute to disruptions in parent-child communication and the cold, hostile tone of the relationship between parent and child. Before his untimely death, Dr. Puig-Antich and his colleagues at the University of Pittsburgh studied patterns of interaction in families of depressed children both before and after the children recovered from a depressive episode. They found that, in many respects, as the child's mood and behavior improved, so did the quality of the parent-child relationship.[14]

These findings suggest that the behavior of depressed youngsters directly affects the way their parents treat them. It is encouraging to find, however, that patterns of parent behavior are not set in cement and that changes in the child's mood and behavior can bring about changes in the parent's behavior.

THE ROLE OF TRAUMA AND STRESS

Since the time of Sigmund Freud behavioral scientists have looked to a person's life experiences to explain the origin of psychological problems. Early experiences—especially traumatic ones—were considered to be particularly important in sowing the seeds of problems which blossom later in life.

TRAUMATIC EVENTS

For many years it was widely believed that the roots of depression lay in an early separation from a parent, a loss so overwhelming that it rendered the child vulnerable to depression for the rest of his life. Subsequent research has shown, however, that it is not so much the loss itself that matters as it is

---

problems can result as the two very different people try to form a mutually satisfying relationship.

the lack of care that often follows such a loss. Children who lose a parent early in life but who are loved and well cared for are at much lower risk for depression in later life than those who suffer indifference and poor care after being separated from the parent.[15]

The extreme of poor care, of course, is abuse. As we would expect, abused children are at high risk for a wide variety of psychiatric disorders, including depression. Children who have been sexually abused seem to be particularly prone to depression, and the onset of the depressive symptoms is likely to be early in life. Certainly not all children who have been sexually abused become depressed or develop psychiatric problems; many other factors are involved, such as the extent of the abuse, the child's relationship with the abuser, and the manner in which parents and others close to the child respond to the incident. The risk is greatest for those who have suffered repeated, severe abuse, especially when the abuse has been perpetrated by a family member or other caretaking adult from whom the child had a right to expect good care.[16]

What about other traumatic or painful experiences which might contribute to depression in children and adolescents? Divorce has been cited as one such experience and, in fact, several researchers have found that parental divorce can result in behavioral disturbances and depression in young people.[17] However, as British psychiatrist Dr. Richard Harrington points out, it is difficult to draw direct connections between parental divorce and depression in young people because there are so many other factors which may be involved. For example, he states, it may not be the actual divorce itself which catapults a youngster into a depressive episode: it could also be the marital conflict which typically precedes a divorce or the consequences which often follow divorce (e.g., changes in residence, school, and family income).[18]

"When my parents finally decided to get a divorce, it was actually kind of a relief because I figured there would

finally be an end to all the fighting and yelling. But then I found out that we would have to move because my mom couldn't afford to keep the house. That meant that I had to change schools and move away from all my friends, too.

"My new school is okay, I guess, but I hate riding the bus and I still miss my old friends. I can't see them after school because, since the divorce, my mom's gone back to work and I have to baby-sit my little sister every day after school. I can't even see my friends on weekends because that's when I go to my dad's house. And that's another problem: I wouldn't want to miss spending time with my dad but it's such a pain to have to get all my stuff together to go over there. I always forget things I'm going to need—makeup, clothes, books, whatever. Then, when I get back to Mom's house on Sunday—sure enough, I've left something at my dad's house!

"I get so tired of all the hassles, I don't know whether to scream or to cry. Sometimes, I even think that maybe all that fighting wasn't so bad after all."

MINOR LIFE EVENTS

As the foregoing example suggests, sometimes it isn't one major stressful event that overwhelms a young person's ability to cope and results in a depressive episode. In many cases, the cumulative effects of minor stressful events that occur on a regular basis can be as much of a psychological burden as a single traumatic event.

At the University of Vermont, Dr. Bruce Compas and his colleagues have examined the relationship between daily stressors and psychological problems, particularly depression. Their research indicates that the connection between daily hassles, such as responsibilities at home and arguments with parents or peers, and the development of a mood disorder is actually stronger than that between a traumatic event and the development of a mood disorder. In fact, Dr. Compas believes that the deleterious effects of traumatic events are due, at least in part, to the fact that they spawn so many minor stressful events which occur repeatedly, as illustrated in the previous example.[19]

Dr. Compas's research may help us understand why some youngsters become depressed and even suicidal following a seemingly minor incident, such as an argument with a friend or the death of a pet goldfish. Often, when we take a close look at the sequence of events in the young person's life, we find that the event, although not particularly traumatic in itself, was just the latest in a long series of disappointments and altercations.

IS IT HEREDITARY?

Does depression "run" in some families, like diabetes and other disorders which have a genetic component? In many families this certainly seems to be the case. As mental health professionals know from experience, depressed children more often than not have at least one parent who also suffers from depression. Conversely, if one parent has depressive disorder, a youngster has about one chance in four of having a similar disorder and, if both parents are afflicted, the risk can be as great as three chances out of four.[20]

Brothers and sisters of depressed youngsters are also more likely than other children to suffer from depression. The risk is greatest for children who have a depressed twin: if one member of a pair of identical twins has depressive illness, there is a 76 percent chance that the other will be affected as well. This risk drops to about 25 percent for fraternal twins and for nontwin brothers and sisters.[21] Nor do other members of the extended family escape: when relatives of depressed children are examined, high rates of depressive illness can often be traced through several generations.

Particularly compelling evidence for the role of heredity

in depressive illness comes from studies of depressed children raised from infancy by parents who were not their biological parents. Several large-scale studies conducted in the United States and abroad[22] have revealed a much higher incidence of depression in the biological relatives of depressed adoptees than in their adoptive families, a pattern which certainly supports the notion of genetic susceptibility in depression.

Other problems also seem to run in the families of depressed children. For example, researchers often find that members of the immediate and extended family are more likely than others in the population to suffer from such psychiatric disorders as alcoholism and anxiety disorders.[23]

What are we to make of these findings? Since many depressed youngsters grow up in families in which one or more members has a psychiatric illness, does this mean that there is a hereditary component in depression? Or should we chalk up the child's problems to the stress of living within a disturbed family?

In years past such questions were debated with much heat but little light or enlightenment by scientists engaged in the so-called "nature versus nurture controversy." As you have probably figured out from the preceding discussion, however, these questions don't have either-or answers. Instead, it appears that many diverse elements interact with each other in a most complex way to determine whether or not a specific individual develops a mood disorder. As we have seen, the caliber of parenting a child receives, the overall quality of family life, the child's own temperament, the interaction of child and parent temperaments, and genetic endowment are all important factors in the equation.

To return to the question of heredity, specifically, we might ask, "What is it that the depressed child inherits?" New research on the brain and behavior, discussed in the following sections, suggests some answers to this question.

IS DEPRESSION CAUSED BY DISTURBANCES IN THE BRAIN?

Parents of depressed youngsters often ask, "Could my child's problems be due to some sort of chemical imbalance in his brain?" Scientists have long suspected that depression does, indeed, result from chemical malfunctions in the brain but, although there have been literally thousands of research studies which have addressed this question, advances in our actual knowledge have come slowly. Progress has been hindered by the incredible complexity of the brain and by our lack of techniques to study it without harming or destroying it. To understand the difficulties neuroscientists face, as well as to understand how brain and behavior are linked, you must first know a bit about the amazing organ that is the human brain.

THE BRAIN AND HOW IT WORKS

We are all aware of the wonders which modern computers can perform, but no computer exists which can match the human brain for complexity of design and flexibility of function. The brain consists of billions of nerve cells. That fact in itself is difficult to comprehend, since it is hard for us to conceive of such vast numbers. Now, add the fact that each nerve cell has hundreds or even thousands of interconnections with other nerve cells: the number of possible interconnections becomes truly mind-boggling. As the pioneering neuroscientist Charles Sherrington so poetically described it, the brain ". . . is a vast enchanted loom with millions of flashing shuttles weaving a dissolving pattern."[24]

Groups of nerve cells form highly specialized control centers in the brain. Fibers extend outward from these centers, forming pathways that link the control centers to each other. Within and between these centers, nerve cells communicate with each other by sending electrical signals through long projections called axons. When the electrical impulse reaches the end of the axon, storage sacs in the nerve endings at the end of the axon release substances known as neurotransmitters—chemical messengers that carry the impulse across the tiny space separating the nerve endings from the body of the next nerve cell. These chemical messengers activate receptors on the body of that cell, causing it to fire in turn.

If you think about this process for a minute, you will see that, after the message has been transmitted and received, the neurotransmitter must somehow be removed from the site or deactivated; otherwise it would continue to send the same message forever. Within the brain, several methods exist to remove these spent chemical messengers. One method is called "re-uptake": the neurotransmitter returns to the sending cell where it is taken up into the storage sacs and saved for future use. The process of chemical breakdown and deactivation is another way in which neurotransmitters are removed from the site.

Neuroscientists have amassed convincing evidence that mental disorders are caused by breakdowns in this complicated chemical messenger system. Depression is just one of the many psychiatric conditions that seem to reflect problems in brain biochemistry.

DEPRESSION AND BRAIN CHEMISTRY

In addition to the neuroendocrine abnormalities we described in Chapter 3, evidence pointing to a biochemical malfunction in depression has come from many other sources over the years, including scientific "flukes" and chance observations.

In the early 1950s, for example, physicians who treated patients for high blood pressure noticed that about 10 percent of patients treated with reserpine, an antihypertensive agent, developed all the symptoms of depression, including loss of appetite, sleep problems, and loss of sexual drive. This was the first solid evidence for a link between brain biochemistry and depression.

At about the same time, other doctors seeking a cure for tuberculosis observed that a new antituberculosis drug, iproniazid, produced significant mood elevation in some patients. This improvement in mood was often quite striking—so striking, in fact, that scientists soon began to investigate the mood-altering properties of the drug. These and subsequent investigations yielded a double payoff: they resulted in the development of an increasingly powerful arsenal of drugs to treat depression (see Chapter 6); and they led to dramatic advances in our understanding of the role neurotransmitters play in depressive illness.

From countless painstaking studies, neuroscientists have learned that the neurotransmitters norepinephrine and serotonin appear to be particularly significant in depression. Serotonin, in particular, makes sense as a factor in mood disorders because it is important in systems which regulate sleep, appetite, motor activity, and aggression, all of which are often disturbed in depressed individuals.

It would be a gross oversimplification to say that we know all about how neurotransmitters function (or, more appropriately **malfunction**) in depression: neuroscientists still have much work to do before that claim can be made. Their search is complicated by the fact that they cannot directly assess neurotransmitters in the human brain, so they must rely on indirect measures, such as levels of neurotransmitter breakdown products in blood, urine, and spinal fluid. This presents problems because, for example, we cannot be certain about what parts of the brain produced which chemical.* Nevertheless, progress to date has been exciting and there is a promise of much more to come in terms of our ability to understand the biological underpinnings of depressive illness.

---

* New brain imaging techniques such as positron emission tomography (PET), single photon emission computed tomography (SPECT), and magnetic resonance imaging (MRI) are sure to be invaluable tools in helping us pinpoint the specific regions of the brain involved in depression.

FIVE

What Can We Do About It?

Psychological Methods of Treatment

WHAT IS PSYCHOTHERAPY?

SOMETIMES CALLED "the talking cure," the word "psychotherapy" encompasses a wide variety of techniques aimed at helping people make changes in their attitudes, emotions, and behavior patterns. To someone unfamiliar with psychotherapy, the word itself calls up the image of a patient lying prone on a couch, while a bearded man with a heavy German accent takes notes and occasionally murmurs, "Umm-hmm" and "I see."

In reality, there are many different "schools," or types, of psychotherapy, each with its own theories and techniques.* In

---

* One researcher found that there are more than **two hundred** different kinds of psychotherapy for children. Is it any wonder that parents are confused when they attempt to find appropriate treatment for their youngsters?

general the major types of psychotherapy fall into four broad categories:

- Those which focus on helping the depressed individual gain an understanding and awareness of the unconscious forces and conflicts which result in depressed mood and behavior. These approaches are best described as insight-oriented therapy.

- Those which directly target changing "depressed" behavior by changing the consequences which are believed to strengthen and weaken behavior. These methods fall under the heading of behavior therapy or behavior modification.

- Those which stress changing maladaptive ways of thinking as a means of changing resulting emotions and behavior. This type of therapy is called cognitive therapy.

- Those which emphasize improving the depressed individual's interpersonal communication skills and his relationships with others. This category includes interpersonal psychotherapy and family therapy.

On the face of it, these approaches appear quite different from one another. In reality, however, there is a great deal of overlap and psychotherapists of all persuasions often borrow freely from different schools in their day-to-day clinical work. Dr. Norman Rosenthal, a psychiatrist who is both a well-known researcher in depression as well as a skilled clinician, uses this colorful analogy to describe the process.

. . . [M]ost skilled therapists combine elements derived from different schools of therapy, much as a skilled chef would combine different ingredients to prepare a gourmet meal.[1]

Further, he states:

> I am generally quite suspicious of people who believe that only
> one narrow school of thought carries the key to curing all
> psychological problems. People are far too diverse and compli-
> cated for such simple solutions.

As practicing clinicians, we certainly agree with Dr. Rosenthal's opinion and we can attest to the truth of his observations. Nevertheless, we think that it is important that you, as a
parent, know a bit about the differences among the various
types of psychotherapy so that you can select the general approach which seems best suited to the needs of your child and
your family.

In this chapter we will provide a brief overview of each of
the major schools of psychotherapy. We will outline the ratio-
nale underlying each and provide a description of the procedures, as well as what we consider to be the pros and cons of
each approach, so that you can make an informed decision for
you and for your child.

TYPES OF PSYCHOTHERAPY

INSIGHT-ORIENTED THERAPY

Insight-oriented therapy is based in large part on the theories
of Sigmund Freud, who is well known to all of us as the father
of psychoanalysis. According to psychoanalytic theory, psychological symptoms of depression and anxiety stem from unacceptable sexual and aggressive impulses and from buried
memories of traumatic experiences such as separation from
the mother, death or loss of a loved one, sexual overstimula-
tion, or great physical pain and suffering. Because these impulses and memories are too awful to be faced head on, they
are repressed, or buried, in the unconscious to protect the individual from overwhelming pain. The problem, however, is
that, even though this buried material is hidden from con-

scious awareness, it remains very much alive below the surface and is the source of a great deal of conflict in the unconscious mind. This underlying conflict, in turn, erupts and emerges as symptoms of psychological distress.

The goal of insight-oriented psychotherapy is to unearth buried material from the unconscious and bring it into the person's conscious awareness. As the person gains awareness ("insight") into this material, he learns that he can confront and master these sources of conflict and can then move on to a healthier, more satisfying adjustment.

How does psychodynamic psychotherapy work? What happens in the therapy sessions? What will your role be as a parent of a youngster in therapy? Insight-oriented therapists focus primarily on working directly with the patient, rather than with family members, so you can expect to meet only occasionally with your child's therapist. In the therapy sessions, the therapist will use a number of techniques to uncover unconscious material and bring it to the surface. He then can interpret this material and subsequently help his patient understand it, come to grips with it, and master it.

With adults and older adolescents, the techniques used by the insight oriented therapist obviously involve a great deal of talking and discussion. The therapist works to help the patient make connections between his current feelings and his past experiences. The process is a long and arduous one as results emerge slowly.

Young children, however, are limited in their ability to use language. Thus child therapists have developed a modified approach known as "play therapy" for use with children who suffer from depression and other psychiatric disorders. In play therapy, the therapist uses play materials, games, and toys to build a working relationship with the child and to establish a setting in which the child feels free to express his feelings.

Play is also used to help the therapist understand the nature of the child's fears, needs, and inner conflicts. Play is then subsequently used as a means of helping the child grapple with and master his difficulties. This ingenious approach to helping young children come to grips with all sorts of life problems has been incorporated as a technique into a variety of other "schools" of psychotherapy, including behavior therapy and cognitive therapy (see pp. 83 and 86).

THE PROS AND CONS. How effective is psychodynamic psychotherapy for the problems of depressed children and adolescents? This is a difficult question to answer. Even with adult patients, the research in this area is hard to interpret. To quote Dr. Rosenthal again:

> Although this type of therapy is extremely difficult to study in a way that meets the rigorous requirements of modern clinical research, it is the experience of trained observers that [it] can be extremely helpful.[2]

This is also the impression of those who have studied the benefits of insight-oriented therapy with children and adolescents.

What are the drawbacks? Insight-oriented therapy is usually a lengthy, expensive process, since therapy sessions are scheduled at least weekly over periods of time which can extend for years. With this approach, parents often complain they are "out of the loop" and have no idea what is actually going on with their child's therapy, since the bulk of the work takes place between the child and his therapist. This is especially likely to be the case when a young child is involved in play therapy, since it is difficult for parents to believe that anything of merit can actually be accomplished when the youngster seems to do little more than draw pictures or crash toy cars into each other.

Older children and adolescents may find the hard work of therapy tedious and not particularly enjoyable. Certainly, if this approach is to be successful, it requires that the young person make a commitment to a lot of hard—sometimes painful—work for a fairly long period of time. While there are some very bright, verbal young people who can make and follow through on such a commitment, in our experience many older children and adolescents find the experience uncomfortable, incomprehensible, and therefore of little help.

Behavior therapy, also called behavior modification, is based on the premise that specific behaviors are learned because they produce specific effects, or consequences. In general, positive consequences—those which are pleasant or enjoyable—tend to strengthen behavior, making it more likely that it will occur again. Thus, a puppy who is rewarded with a pat and a treat learns to come when he is called and a toddler learns to say "Please" if this behavior results in a cookie.

If no consequences follow on the heels of a particular behavior—if, for example, you repeatedly deposit coins in a vending machine but receive nothing in return—the behavior weakens and dies out (i.e., you no longer deposit coins in the machine). This process occurs even more rapidly when negative, or punishing, consequences follow the behavior; if, for example, you receive a nasty shock each time you deposit coins in the slot of the vending machine, you will quickly cease your efforts to obtain a snack or a drink from that machine.

Consequences, also called *reinforcers*, need not be dramatic in order to have an effect on behavior. In fact, some consequences such as a praise, a smile, or a frown can be surprisingly effective in strengthening or weakening behavior. Timing, however, is critical: behavior is affected most powerfully by consequences which immediately follow the behavior.

How has this knowledge been applied to the treatment of emotional and behavioral problems? Using principles of reinforcement, the therapist can systematically arrange events so that positive consequences follow, and thereby strengthen, behaviors the therapist wishes to increase. At the same time, undesirable behaviors can be weakened and eliminated by ensuring that they are never followed by positive consequences or by following them quickly with negative consequences. Using this approach, behavior therapists have been able to treat an impressive array of problem behaviors in children and adults suffering from psychiatric disorders.

With individuals suffering from depression, behavior therapy techniques have been used to, among other things, reduce social isolation and increase social interaction, as well as to produce increases in other kinds of adaptive behaviors. This approach has been shown to be at least somewhat helpful in treating depression, especially when it is combined with other techniques to help depressed patients gain access to sources of positive reinforcement, such as social skills training and cognitive therapy (see p. 86).

In addition to their work with reinforcement procedures, behavior therapists have also developed fear-reduction techniques. These techniques consist of repeatedly pairing a pleasant event with something that causes fear or emotional arousal to bring about changes in emotional responding and, subsequently, behavior. As long ago as the mid-twenties, for example, a youngster who was terrified of rabbits was cured of his fear in short order when the object of his fear—a rabbit—was gradually brought closer and closer while the youngster was happily engaged in eating his favorite food.

Almost forty years ago pioneering psychiatrist Dr. Joseph Wolpe at Temple University refined this approach into a technique which came to be known as *systematic desensitization.*[3] This technique involves training the patient in techniques of deep muscle relaxation and then gradually presenting the feared object (either real or in the patient's imagination) while the patient is relaxed and comfortable. With children, teaching the child to imagine himself engaged in enjoyable or exciting activities is often substituted for relaxation procedures. Systematic desensitization is the most widely used and intensively researched treatment method for reducing irrational fears and it has been employed successfully in the treatment of fears and phobias in both children and adults.

Behavior therapy approaches to the treatment of school refusal, a common problem with depressed youngsters, offer a good example of how behavioral principles can be applied to some of the specific problems experienced by these children. A treatment program for this problem might include the following components:

- Reducing anxiety about school attendance through the use of systematic desensitization.

- Providing positive consequences for school attendance (e.g., school attendance earns child points toward enjoyable activities, privileges, or material goods).

- Replacing positive consequences for school avoidance with negative consequences (e.g., if child remains at home for a day, he must remain in his room, with no access to enjoyable activities).

THE PROS AND CONS. There is a large and quite convincing body of evidence that behavioral methods can be very helpful for specific problems such as school refusal and other anxiety-based kinds of difficulties. There is also evidence to indicate that behavior therapy can be effective in reducing other problem behaviors associated with depression, such as social withdrawal, temper tantrums, and poor school performance.

The scope of behavior therapy is limited: behavioral techniques alone cannot offer a comprehensive treatment program for depression. However, behavioral techniques such as modeling, rehearsal, self-monitoring, and rearranging consequences are important components of other forms of treatment, especially cognitive therapy (see p. 86).

Finally, behavior management programs based on these principles and techniques can be very helpful on the home front and in the classroom. A large body of literature attests to the fact that parents and teachers can be taught to apply these principles in successful behavior change programs, as we discuss in Chapters 8 and 9.

Cognitive therapy has its roots in the groundbreaking work of Dr. Aaron Beck, a psychiatrist at the University of Pennsylvania.[4] According to Dr. Beck, people who suffer from depression develop *cognitive distortions,* or maladaptive ways of thinking about themselves, the world, and the future. These negatively toned thoughts (which we referred to earlier as "looking at the world through mud-colored glasses") in turn lead to feelings of depression and despair. What are these cognitive distortions?

- **Negative self-evaluation:** Depressed people believe that they are defective and unworthy, lacking in what it takes to be successful and happy. They are highly self-critical and quick to blame themselves for any misfortune that comes their way.

- **Negative worldview:** Depressed people seem to have a special knack for interpreting ongoing events in the worst possible light. They often misinterpret the actions of others, taking offense at every tiny slight and attributing malice when none was intended.

- **Negative view of the future:** When depressed people look ahead, they are sure that the future will be at least as bleak as the present, if not more so. To them, the light at the end of the tunnel is just the headlights of a train coming at them!

The development of cognitive therapy also owes a debt to Dr. Albert Ellis, father of **rational-emotive therapy.**[5] In Dr. Ellis's view, people develop irrational, self-defeating beliefs which inevitably result in negative emotions, such as rage, guilt, anxiety, and depression. High on the list of irrational ideas which lead to disturbed feelings and emotions is the belief that it is a dire necessity to have the love or approval of everyone with whom one comes in contact. This is clearly an impossibility, since some people may dislike us simply because of the color of our eyes or skin or hair—or just because they are in a lousy mood at the moment! Another irrational belief which has direct ties to depression is the idea that one must be completely competent and achieving in all possible respects. Again, this is obviously impossible, since who among us can claim to be perfect in every endeavor we undertake?

Researchers who have studied the thought patterns and beliefs of depressed individuals tell us that negative bias and cognitive distortions accompany depressive illness in both adults and children.[6] Cognitive therapy techniques, designed to help depressed youngsters identify and alter these maladaptive ways of thinking, include the following:

- **Cognitive restructuring:** Depressed youngsters are taught to identify specific negative thoughts and beliefs which result in feelings of depression and despair (e.g., "Even if I try my best, I will fail"). They are then helped to challenge the accuracy of these thoughts (e.g., "I believe that even if I try my best I will fail. Has that always happened? Have I ever succeeded?") and to generate more adaptive alternatives (e.g., "If I try my best, I might fail, but I also might succeed!").

- **Attribution training:** The word "attribution" refers to the way in which we explain the things that happen to us in life. People who attribute their successes to their own skills and efforts rather than to outside forces such as luck are said to have an **internal locus of control.** Depressed people often have an **external locus of control;** that is, they blame themselves for all the bad things that happen to them but write off any achievements or successes as due to happenstance. The process of attribution training involves teaching depressed youngsters to choose more adaptive attributions and to use them to solve problems more effectively.

- **Self-control training:** To help them change negative and maladaptive patterns of thinking, depressed youngsters are taught to monitor and evaluate their thoughts on an ongoing basis. They are also taught to reward themselves for doing this, in order to strengthen the new patterns.

- **Adjunctive techniques:** Since depressed youngsters usually have other problems in addition to maladaptive patterns of thinking, most cognitive therapy programs include adjunctive components specifically aimed at these problems. To help youngsters with social skills deficits, for example, social skills training offers an opportunity to learn and practice a variety of social and communication skills, such as how to initiate social contacts, how to make new friends, and how to negotiate and problem-solve in interpersonal relationships.

An excellent example of a comprehensive cognitive treatment program for depressed adolescents is the "Adolescent Coping with Depression Course," developed by Dr. Peter Lewinsohn and his colleagues at the University of Oregon Health Sciences Center. This program consists of sixteen two-hour sessions, conducted in groups of four to eight teenagers. Through lectures, discussions, role play, and homework assignments, participants learn a variety of skills, including how to alter negative thought patterns, how to improve social skills and communication with others, more effective problem-solving skills, and relaxation techniques. Dr. Lewinsohn's research has shown that more than 70 percent of depressed adolescents treated with this program are significantly improved at the end of treatment and that gains are maintained for up to a year afterward.[7]

THE PROS AND CONS. Dr. Lewinsohn's research and that

of others certainly suggests that cognitive therapy offers a very promising method for treating depression in young people. The brevity of the treatment is likely to appeal to teenagers, many of whom may be reluctant to make long-term commitments to treatment. The nature of the treatment itself—a structured, directive approach which puts the youngster in the role of colleague rather than patient—is also a plus, since adolescents often resist the role of patient as a "one-down" position.

It is important to point out, however, that cognitive therapy has not been verified as an effective treatment for suicidal youngsters[*8] or those with coexisting problems such as conduct disorder, substance abuse, personality disorders, or learning disabilities. Since, as we have discussed, many depressed youngsters have one or more coexisting conditions, the number of youngsters who might benefit from cognitive treatment may be somewhat smaller than would appear at first glance.

We should also note that most of the outcome studies conducted so far have been concerned with group treatments for depressive disorders. While group therapy has often been touted as a particularly useful format for teenagers, in practice it is difficult to set up groups in most outpatient clinics, since the number of depressed teenagers at any one time is likely to be small.

Finally, although it is claimed that cognitive therapy approaches can be used effectively with children as young as ten years of age, the efficacy of this approach has not been tested with children much below the age of fourteen. Recent attempts to combine elements of cognitive therapy with play therapy for use with younger children are intriguing, but research which supports this as a useful intervention with depressed children is not yet available.[9]

---

* Tests of a cognitive therapy program known as SNAP are now under way at Columbia University with adolescents who have attempted suicide. Preliminary results are encouraging. (See Note 8.)

COMMUNICATION/RELATIONSHIP THERAPY

FAMILY THERAPY. The term "family therapy" is particularly confusing to many parents who, having heard the term, assume that it means simply that parents are included and actively involved in the child's treatment. Since parents of depressed youngsters are so often acutely aware of the disturbed patterns of interaction among family members, a therapy program which addresses these problems is particularly appealing.

What most parents do not realize, however, is that "family therapy" refers not just to sessions in which family members participate together, but to specific approaches to treatment known as "strategic family therapy" and "structural family therapy." Therapists trained in these schools view the child's problem as a reflection of disturbances in the way the family operates. There may, for example, be hidden marital problems which are related to the youngster's problems. It may also be the case that parents have abdicated their rightful roles as authority figures or that one parent has formed an alliance with the child against the other parent.

Treatment is aimed at correcting these disturbances by improving communication among all family members, teaching problem-solving skills, and helping parents reestablish their positions as authority figures in the household. Depending on their particular training, family therapists also use a variety of other techniques to restore equilibrium to the dysfunctional family. In so doing, it is assumed, the depressed youngster will gradually improve as family functioning improves.

THE PROS AND CONS. Family therapy is usually a brief, action-oriented approach. On the face of it, it would certainly seem to be an ideal approach to treating the problems of depressed children since there are often high levels of conflict in the families of these children.

Unfortunately, while there have been several studies evaluating family therapy as a treatment for general family dysfunction, there have been no studies which have looked specifically at the use of family therapy for depressed children and adolescents. As is the case with insight-oriented therapy, it is difficult to study the effectiveness of this approach in a controlled scientific manner although there are anecdotal reports that this approach can be helpful to some depressed youngsters and their families.

Parents should be aware, however, that young people—particularly teenagers—are sometimes reluctant to attend and participate cooperatively in family therapy sessions. Unless the therapist is very skilled and tactful, sessions can deteriorate into shouting matches which leave bad feelings on all sides. There is also the danger that, with the emphasis on the family as a whole, the specific problems of the depressed child will be overlooked and therefore go untreated.

INTERPERSONAL PSYCHOTHERAPY. Interpersonal psychotherapy (IPT) is a time-limited, brief (twelve to sixteen weeks) form of therapy originally designed specifically for the treatment of depression in adults. It has since been modified for use with depressed adolescents by Doctors Laura Mufson and Donna Moreau at Columbia University, who have also conducted tests of its effectiveness as a treatment method for these youngsters.

IPT is based on the premise that depression occurs, not in a vacuum, but within the context of the ongoing interpersonal relationships in the patient's life. The goals of IPT are to identify and treat the adolescent's depressive symptoms as well as the problem areas associated with the onset of the depressive episode. With depressed youngsters, these problem areas include the following:

- **Prolonged grief:** The youngster has suffered the loss of an important relationship, such as a family member or a friend, and has become depressed as a result.

- **Interpersonal role disputes:** The young person and his parents disagree on important issues such as sexual behavior, authority, money, and life values.

- **Role transitions:** The young person has difficulty with changes in demands and expectations as he progresses from one developmental stage to the next (e.g., entering puberty, moving away from home).

- **Interpersonal deficits:** The youngster lacks the necessary social skills to establish satisfying relationships with others, both within and outside the family.

- **Single-parent family issues:** When a family is separated by death, divorce, or incarceration, the young person must grapple with his reactions to the event.

In IPT, the therapist helps the adolescent understand how problems with interpersonal relationships directly affect his emotions. Emphasis is placed on current relationships, rather than those which existed in the past. Using such techniques as rehearsal and role play, the therapist helps the youngster learn to talk about his emotions rather than "act out" feelings through depressed, antisocial, or self-punishing behavior. On occasion, the therapist may meet with the adolescent and his parents to clarify mutual expectations and to support the adolescent in expressing his point of view in an appropriate, forthright manner.

THE PROS AND CONS. As a treatment for mildly to moderately depressed adolescents, IPT would certainly seem to have much to offer. Doctors Mufson and Moreau rightly point out that a focus on identifying and resolving interpersonal disputes seems very appropriate for adolescents, since they are often in disputes with parents, schools, or friends. They also note that, because adolescence is a time when major life choices are being established, a treatment that helps the young person identify and master interpersonal problems is timely and provides valuable skills for the future. Finally, they add, young people are often reluctant to enter into lengthy treatment contracts, so a treatment approach that is brief and time-limited seems tailor-made for teenagers.

How effective is IPT? The originators of IPT, Dr. Myrna Weissman and the late Dr. Gerald Klerman, were not only talented clinicians but conscientious scientists who understood the need to subject new treatment methods to careful scientific scrutiny. To date, IPT has been tested and shown to be quite effective with depressed adults in several clinical trials.[10]

Studies of the effectiveness of IPT with depressed adolescents are now under way, under the direction of Doctors Mufson and Moreau. Early results are promising indeed: after only twelve weeks of treatment, a group of depressed teenagers showed significant improvement in a number of areas of functioning and in depressive symptoms. In fact, at the end of this brief treatment, 90 percent could no longer be considered depressed.[11]

These are, indeed, exciting findings. However, as Dr. Richard Harrington points out, one caveat is in order. IPT, he notes, "was developed for nonpsychotic, nonsuicidal depressed adolescent outpatients who were not engaging in regular drug use or antisocial activities of a violent nature: it was not designed to handle 'adolescents in crisis.' "[12] As with cognitive therapy, then, IPT may not be effective with all depressed youngsters.

LOCATING AND WORKING WITH A THERAPIST

As a parent, how do you go about finding a therapist who is skilled in working with the problems of depressed children and adolescents? How can you be sure that the therapist will be a good "match" for your child and for your family? What can you expect of the therapist and what will be expected of you?

SELECTING A THERAPIST

In Chapter 3 we outlined the ways in which parents should go about obtaining the services of a competent professional to evaluate their child. In most cases, the professional who conducts the evaluation will also be able to provide therapy for the child or, alternatively, will be able to refer you to a competent professional for therapy.

If the professional who conducts the evaluation is for some reason unable to treat the child in therapy or refer you to a competent professional for therapy, you should follow the steps described in Chapter 3 to find a skilled mental health professional to work with your child.

When it comes to who is best qualified to treat your depressed youngster, the letters after the person's name (e.g., M.D., Ph.D., L.C.S.W.) are not as important as how much experience the professional has had in working with youngsters like yours and how comfortable you are with the therapist's style, personality, and general orientation.

Don't be discouraged if a particular type of treatment does not seem to be readily available in your community. Call your local mental health agency or the state professional associations (psychological, psychiatric, social work) in your state for information. State colleges and universities—especially those with medical schools—are often good sources of information as well. In some cases, if there is an ongoing research program dealing with childhood depression, treatment may be available free of charge if your child meets the criteria for entry into the study.

WORKING WITH A THERAPIST

As practicing clinicians, we have found that a mismatch between what parents and mental health professionals expect from the relationship can lead to misunderstandings and problems in the child's treatment. Sometimes, for example, parents adopt a "hands-off" attitude toward the child's treatment, limiting their involvement to taking the child to the appointments and paying the bills. This is a serious mistake because parents can provide important information about how the child functions on a day-to-day basis. Since they are with the child so much of the time, they can also serve as very powerful agents of behavior change for the youngsters if they are actively involved in the treatment.

But problems can arise in the other direction as well: it sometimes happens that parents expect to have access to more information than the therapist can provide, given the rules which govern therapist-patient confidentiality. As we noted in Chapter 3, all therapists, including those who treat young people, are bound by their ethical code to protect the privacy of their patients. This means that the therapist can (and should) keep you informed about your child's general progress but that he or she is not at liberty to divulge specific information (e.g., whether or not the youngster is sexually active) unless the youngster's behavior presents a definite danger to himself or others. As a parent, you might find this "limited information" policy frustrating but, without it, little could be accomplished in the child's therapy.

Finally, problems can occur if parents don't understand the fact that, since the only "product" therapists have to sell is their time, they must bill for the time they spend on behalf of their patients. This means that they must bill for missed appointments, except in cases of true emergencies; for meetings attended on the child's behalf; and even for telephone time (although most therapists do not charge for brief telephone calls). If you have to have a lengthy conversation with your child's therapist, schedule an office appointment, since most insurance companies will not reimburse you for telephone sessions.

We have found that many of the problems discussed above can be avoided if there is a clear understanding, up front, as to what parents and therapist can expect from each other. If questions arise, don't be afraid to discuss them openly. Only when parents and therapist work together as a team can we expect optimum benefit for the child.

Psychotherapy is a labor-intensive service provided by highly trained professionals. As a result, it is costly. Depending on geographic location and the type of mental health professional conducting the therapy, rates for a 45- to 50-minute session range from $60 to more than $200.

Parents are often unpleasantly surprised to find that their insurance plan covers little of the cost involved in mental health care. In fact, insurance companies have routinely practiced discrimination against people with psychiatric disorders through such tactics as limiting the number of mental health visits during the course of a year and placing a lifetime "cap" on the total amount the insurance company will expend on psychiatric treatment for an individual. Most insurance plans also have higher patient co-payment requirements for mental health services than for other medical services; thus, while you might be expected to pay only 20 percent of the cost of a visit to a pediatrician, an orthopedist, or a gynecologist, your share of the cost for mental health visits is likely to be as high as 50 percent.

There is some reason to hope that new reform legislation will provide nondiscriminatory coverage for mental health care so that mental health visits will be covered at the same rate that applies to other medical services. However, while this would reduce "sticker shock" for families with more traditional forms of insurance, it would do nothing to help families who belong to preferred provider and health maintenance organizations (PPOs and HMOs), because these families face a different set of problems. In HMOs and PPOs, parents must first fight their way through a maze of advice nurses, family practitioners, and pediatricians just to obtain *permission to make an appointment* with a mental health provider who is in the plan. After this battle—which can be very protracted and quite frustrating—parents still have little or no choice as to the professional who will work with them and with their child. Certainly, there are many competent and well-qualified professionals who are in the employ of these systems. However, if the match between the professional and your child is poor, or if the professional has little expertise in dealing with your child's specific problems, you will have little recourse but to pay the full fee for alternatives which are not covered financially by the HMO or the PPO.

The answer to this dilemma? We wish we could offer a pat solution but we cannot. Over the long term, we believe that change can come about if parents join forces for legislative change by becoming active in organizations such as NAMI-CAN (see our discussion of "What Lies Ahead" in Chapter 10). In the short run, however, we can only suggest that you view the cost of your child's mental health care as a major investment in the child's future.

SIX

What Else Can We Do About It?

Medical Treatment of Depression

ANTIDEPRESSANT MEDICATIONS

LIKE SO MANY EVENTS in the history of medicine, the discovery of some of the medications which are now used to treat mood disorders came about by happy accident. As we described in Chapter 4, for example, scientists seeking a cure for tuberculosis discovered that the drug iproniazid produced clear and unmistakable improvements in mood in some patients. When this drug was subsequently tested on patients suffering from severe depression, the results were exciting. It was not long before researchers in various laboratories in this country and abroad were working feverishly to develop new and improved drugs for the treatment of depression and other psychiatric illnesses. The boom was on! Now, psychiatrists have a broad array of antidepressant medications available to them, with many more "in the pipeline."

HOW DO ANTIDEPRESSANTS WORK IN THE BRAIN?

Although antidepressant medications have been called "mood elevators," this term is misleading. These medications are not "happy pills": people who take them don't walk around wearing goofy grins and beatific smiles, impervious to the problems of everyday life.

Instead, antidepressant medications are more properly described as "mood regulators," since they seem to restore **normal** functioning by correcting malfunctions in the chemical messenger systems in the brain. Different antidepressants apparently work in different ways to correct neurochemical problems, including the following:

- Some medications exert their beneficial effects by interfering with too rapid breakdown of the brain's own natural neurotransmitters, so that they can remain in place and continue to serve their functions. The drug iproniazid is an example of such a medication.

- Other drugs seem to mimic the action of natural neurotransmitters or increase the rate at which specific neurotransmitters are released from the "sending" nerve cells, so that more of the substance is available in the brain.

- Some very effective antidepressants, such as the tricyclics and the SSRIs (see pp. 100 and 104), appear to prevent the "re-uptake" of certain neurotransmitters; that is, they prevent these chemical messengers from being reabsorbed or taken up by their parent neurons. Again, the net result is that more of the natural chemical substance is available in the brain, for longer periods of time.

- Another way in which some antidepressants affect brain activity is by influencing the sensitivity of particular receptors, making them more or less responsive to incoming messages.

TYPES OF ANTIDEPRESSANT MEDICATIONS

TRICYCLIC ANTIDEPRESSANTS

Tricyclic antidepressants have been in use since the 1950s and, of the many drugs that have been used in the treatment of depression, they have been the most extensively studied in both children and adults. The tricyclics which have been most commonly used with children are imipramine (Tofranil)* and desipramine (Norpramin). Others which have been studied in the treatment of childhood depression include nortriptyline (Pamelor) and amoxapine (Asendin).

As a treatment for depression in adults, tricyclics have a long and honorable history. They are particularly efficacious in the treatment of moderately severe to severe depression characterized by sleep problems, poor appetite and weight loss, and lethargy.

Early research involving the use of tricyclics with children also gave cause for great optimism. In 1971, for example, Doctors Rachel Gittelman-Klein and Donald Klein, groundbreaking researchers at Columbia University, reported that imipramine was very effective in the treatment of school refusal and other symptoms of anxiety and depression.[1] Other studies subsequently appeared, indicating that tricyclics benefited up to two thirds of children and adolescents suffering from depression.[2]

After such a promising start, it was quite a surprise when the results of controlled studies seemed to indicate that the tricyclics were less helpful in children than in adults—especially since so many practicing clinicians could testify many

* In this chapter, we follow the usual medical practice of identifying the medication by giving the generic name first, followed (in parentheses) by the more commonly known brand name.

times over to the beneficial effects of tricyclics in the treatment of childhood depression. So great was the surprise, in fact, that in July 1990 the National Institute of Mental Health convened a panel of experts to examine the issue. Under the direction of Dr. Peter Jensen, the panel explored myriad questions and possibilities. Perhaps, it was suggested, different biological systems underlie childhood and adult depression: for example, might early-onset depressive illness be more serotonin-based than depressive illness in adults? Or perhaps childhood-onset depression constitutes a more severe form of the disorder than depression which does not emerge until the adult years. Maybe, too, there are different subtypes of depression in children which respond differently to different kinds of medication. In adults, for example, we know that depressions which are characterized by lethargy, overeating, and excessive sleeping are less likely to respond to treatment with tricyclics than other subtypes of depression in which these features are absent. Along these lines, some scientists have suggested that mood disorders that begin early in life are really the early stages of bipolar illness and we know that people with bipolar illness usually do not respond well to treatment with tricyclics alone.* Then, too, perhaps the studies failed to show significant benefit of medication because they were so short in duration: in one study, for example, recovery rates jumped by almost 50 percent when treatment was extended to ten weeks instead of the six-week period more commonly used in drug studies.[3]

To date, we are still waiting for definitive answers to these questions. In the interim, what can we conclude? We agree with Dr. Paul Ambrosini and his colleagues at the Medical College of Pennsylvania, who recently reviewed the research on the subject.[4] They concluded that the clinical use of tricyclics in depressed children and adolescents who do not re-

---

* In fact, there is good evidence that tricyclic antidepressants can actually "uncover" manic episodes in people who have bipolar illness.

spond to nonpharmacological interventions appears warranted, since more than half of those who are treated will have
a favorable response. We agree, too, with their suggestion that
medication should be continued for eight to ten weeks before
making a decision about its effectiveness for a particular child.
Finally, we certainly agree with the consensus among professionals that tricyclics, like all psychotropic medications, work
best when they are part of a comprehensive treatment program which includes other interventions, such as psychotherapy and family counseling.

PROS AND CONS. Although tricyclic antidepressants are
often helpful in treating depressed youngsters, the benefits
may not be obtained without some cost. Many youngsters find
the side effects, such as dry mouth and constipation, so unpleasant that they discontinue use of the medication.

Even if side effects pose problems at higher doses, tricyclics may still be very useful **adjunctive** medications: when
they are combined with other medications and used in low to
moderate doses to target very specific symptoms, they can be
quite helpful in treating youngsters who suffer from mood
disorders.

No matter how small the dose, when tricyclics are prescribed certain precautions must be observed. Since these
medications can affect the electrical activity of the heart, an
EKG (electrocardiogram) should be obtained before beginning
treatment. Also, because it takes some time for the body to
adjust to tricyclics, they should never be stopped abruptly: to
do so can result in flulike symptoms of nausea, stomach pain,
vomiting, and headaches. Finally, parents need to know that
the tricyclics are extremely dangerous when taken in overdose
—much more so than many other prescription and nonpre-
scription drugs. This means that these medicines should always be kept securely beyond the reach of inquisitive toddlers
and they should certainly be locked away from potentially
suicidal teenagers.

MONOAMINE OXIDASE INHIBITORS

Monoamine oxidase inhibitors, abbreviated as MAOIs, are descendants of iproniazid, the drug which produced such improvements in mood in patients suffering from tuberculosis. Commonly used MAOIs include phenelzine (Nardil) and tranylcypromine (Parnate). As we noted above, these drugs are believed to exert their effects by preventing the breakdown of certain neurotransmitters, so that more of these chemical messengers remain available to carry messages from one cell or group of cells to another.

These medications have been widely studied in the treatment of adult depression. They have been shown to be particularly helpful with people who suffer from so-called "atypical" depressions; that is, depressive episodes characterized by excessive eating and sleeping, anxiety, deterioration in mood and energy across the course of the day, and oversensitivity to perceived slights and rejections.

A major drawback of MAOIs is the fact that patients who take them must scrupulously avoid foods rich in tyramine, such as aged cheese, processed meats, wine, and beer. Certain drugs, such as nasal decongestants and cough medicines, must also be avoided. Otherwise, patients risk a serious—even fatal —reaction which includes severely elevated blood pressure, vomiting, headache, and chest pain.

Since young people cannot always be trusted to avoid the temptations of pepperoni pizza (not to mention contraband beer or wine), the risk that MAOIs pose for this age group is clear. It is not surprising that, although the few studies that have been published have reported good results, there has been little enthusiasm for investigating the usefulness of MAOIs as a treatment for depressed children and adolescents.

THE PROS AND CONS. At this time the MAOIs which are currently available are not generally used to treat depression in young people, since the risks are so great. However, research is now under way on monoamine oxidase inhibitors which are much safer to use. These "reversible" MAOIs have not yet been studied in depressed children and adolescents, so whether or not they will be helpful remains to be seen.[5]

SELECTIVE SEROTONIN RE-UPTAKE INHIBITORS

These drugs, known as SSRIs, are the newest of the drugs used to treat depression. Among the SSRIs, fluoxetine (Prozac) is certainly the best known; in fact, it has received so much media publicity that it has become a veritable household word. Other SSRIs available in the United States are sertraline (Zoloft) and paroxetine (Paxil). As the name implies, these drugs are believed to work by preventing re-uptake of the neurotransmitter serotonin.

An important advantage of the SSRIs is that they have few serious side effects. Some patients do report headaches, nausea, or anxiety but these problems are usually mild and time-limited and, when necessary, they can be minimized by reducing the dose. SSRIs are also relatively safe if they are accidentally or deliberately taken in overdose: patients have survived after having taken amounts equal to at least ten times the daily dose.[6]

Prozac and its sister SSRIs appear to offer particular hope in the treatment of depression in young people because, as we have discussed, serotonin systems may play a very important role in childhood depression. There is also evidence from adult studies that SSRIs are effective in depressed patients with characteristics similar to those seen in childhood depression; that is, early age of onset, chronic course of illness, and poor response to tricyclics.[7]

The results of early studies are, in fact, quite promising. In Pittsburgh, Dr. Neal Ryan and his associates at the University of Pittsburgh have amassed evidence for the utility of Prozac in depressed children and adolescents,[8] as have Doctors Carolyn Boulos and Stan Kutcher at the University of

Toronto.[9] In Dallas, Dr. Graham Emslie's group at the University of Texas Southwestern Medical Center has just completed a controlled study of Prozac with depressed youngsters. Their preliminary findings are that this medication is both safe and effective for the treatment of mood disorders in children and adolescents.

Controlled studies of other SSRIs are now under way at various sites in the United States and Canada. Dr. Jovan Simeon's group at the University of Ottawa is conducting a study of Zoloft. Multisite studies of Zoloft are also under way at other research centers as well. In addition, the SSRI fluvoxamine, not yet approved for use in this country, has been tested abroad with depressed youngsters and early results give reason for optimism.[10]

SSRIs also seem to be helpful in treating childhood anxiety disorders which, as we noted, are commonly associated with mood disorders in children and adolescents. In studies at the University of Pittsburgh[11] and the National Institute of Mental Health,[12] researchers have reported that Prozac appeared to be effective and well tolerated in children between the ages of six and seventeen who suffered from a variety of anxiety disorders. Studies conducted at Yale University also indicated that Prozac is generally safe, well tolerated, and effective for the treatment of Obsessive-Compulsive Disorder in children and adolescents.[13] These findings are particularly encouraging, since other medications have proved rather disappointing with anxiety-disordered youngsters (see p. 108).

THE PROS AND CONS. The success of Prozac in the treatment of adult depression has made it so popular that, paradoxically, some people are leery of it on that very basis. "It's so trendy—so yuppie," one parent explained, while another referred to it as "the drug of the month."

The popularity of Prozac has also made it the target of antipsychiatry cults, such as the Church of Scientology. These factions were quick to pounce on reports that suicidal thoughts and preoccupations were reported in a handful of

106 — Lonely, Sad and Angry

patients treated with Prozac. PROZAC: KILLER DRUG? screamed the headlines. Although several careful scientific analyses subsequently indicated that depressed patients are no more likely to become suicidal on Prozac than on any other medication,[14] the damage had been done and many people who might benefit greatly from Prozac have hesitated to use the medication because of lingering concerns about its safety.

As clinicians and scientists, we can only deplore this state of affairs. On the basis of currently available evidence, we believe that Prozac and other SSRIs offer a safe and promising approach to the treatment of depression in children, adolescents, and adults. Don't rely on questionable sources of information: TV talk-show hosts don't qualify as experts, nor does your sister-in-law's neighbor! Instead, we urge you to get up-to-date information about these medications from qualified, experienced mental health professionals who work with medication on a regular basis.

LITHIUM

The history of lithium in the treatment of mood disorders is a long one indeed: almost two thousand years ago the physician Soranus of Ephesus prescribed mineral water for the treatment of conditions we would now call depression and bipolar illness.* Spas—health resorts in which mineral water is an important part of the treatment regimen—have been popular for centuries among people suffering from a variety of chronic physical and mental conditions, depression among them. Today we know that the alkaline springs which feed many of these spas contain high levels of lithium.

But it was not by investigating the properties of mineral water that lithium was introduced into modern medicine. In-

---

* For other interesting information about the history and use of lithium, we recommend Dr. Ronald Fieve's book, *Moodswing* (New York: Bantam Books, 1989).

stead, in the 1940s Australian psychiatrist John Cade discovered the mood-altering properties of this simple salt quite by accident while searching for "toxins" that were believed to cause manic-depressive illness. Dr. Cade's remarkable discovery was largely overlooked by American psychiatrists in the flurry of excitement over the new tranquilizers and antipsychotic drugs then appearing, and it was not until 1970 that lithium was given FDA approval for use in the treatment of manic-depressive illness.

Unlike other, more chemically complicated medications used to treat mood disorders, lithium is a simple, naturally occurring salt. For such a simple substance, lithium appears to exert its effects on the brain in ways so complex that they are as yet not fully understood. Nevertheless, the effects are very powerful: about 80 percent of manic-depressive adults treated with lithium respond favorably.

In addition to its documented effectiveness in controlling manic episodes, lithium also appears to be a good prophylactic agent: when taken on a maintenance basis, it helps prevent or decrease relapses. Researchers have also found that, in some depressed patients who do not respond to treatment with tricyclics, lithium can be used to augment, or "boost," the effects of the tricyclic, resulting in significant improvement in symptoms.

Although more than 16,000 articles on lithium have been published to date, only 58 of these have reported on the use of lithium in children and adolescents.[15] In spite of these small numbers, however, there is compelling evidence that lithium is a very effective treatment for many youngsters who suffer from bipolar illness. There is also a small but convincing body of evidence that lithium is helpful in reducing highly aggressive behavior when all else has failed.[16]

PROS AND CONS. Lithium can certainly be a useful drug in the management of depression and related disorders in children and adolescents. Nevertheless, it is not an easy drug to use. There is a somewhat narrow margin of safety between therapeutic levels and toxic levels so drug levels must be monitored closely. Unfortunately, this involves regular blood tests, which many children find highly objectionable. In addition, although many children tolerate the medication well—better than adults, in fact—some complain of side effects such as weight gain, stomach upset, and fatigue. Finally, lithium can affect thyroid and kidney functioning and the consequences of long-term use in children are as yet unclear.

For these reasons, some child psychiatrists prefer to use the anticonvulsant medications carbamazepine (Tegretol) or valproic acid (Depakene) instead of lithium. These drugs have many of the beneficial effects of lithium but fewer side effects. They have long been used to treat seizure disorders in children and adolescents, so there is also a greater body of accumulated knowledge about them.

ANTIANXIETY MEDICATIONS

The group of antianxiety drugs known as "benzodiazepines" includes the older drugs diazepam (Valium) and chlordiazepoxide (Librium), as well as the newer drugs alprazolam (Xanax) and clonazepam (Klonopin). In the 1970s the benzodiazepines were the most frequently prescribed drugs in the United States until heated controversy over their use followed publicity about their abuse by people who abused alcohol and illegal drugs such as cocaine. In 1990, however, a task force appointed by the American Psychiatric Association concluded that benzodiazepines, "when prescribed appropriately, are therapeutic drugs with relatively mild toxic profiles and low tendency for abuse."[17]

The newer antianxiety medications Xanax and Klonopin have been found to be quite useful in the treatment of adult anxiety disorders. In children, however, the results of rather sparse research indicate that, when these medications are used alone, they may not be particularly helpful in treating children and adolescents with anxiety disorders.[18] In some cases, though, they may be helpful in combination with other medications, especially on a short-term basis.

Buspirone (BuSpar) is a relatively new drug that is not related to the benzodiazepines. It has been shown to be an effective anti-anxiety agent for adults suffering from anxiety disorders, and it may also have a mild antidepressant effect. Although no controlled studies have been done, recent pilot studies at the University of Toronto and the University of Ottawa suggest that BuSpar, alone or in combination with other medications, is useful in treating a variety of anxiety disorders in children and adolescents.[19]

PROS AND CONS. BuSpar appears to be less sedating than the benzodiazepines and no evidence of physical dependence or a withdrawal syndrome has been reported. BuSpar also does not appear to have adverse effects on memory, motor skills, or general intellectual functioning. Children who are treated with benzodiazepines do not seem to become addicted to these medications, nor are there dangerous side effects, especially when medication is used in relatively low doses as a supplemental medication. At higher doses, however, side effects of irritability, mood swings, emotional outbursts, and oppositional behavior can occur. These side effect are most likely to occur in youngsters who are aggressive, impulsive, and under environmental stress.[20]

In children, as in adults, benzodiazepines should never be discontinued abruptly. Otherwise, insomnia is likely to be a problem. At higher doses, abrupt discontinuation of medication can result in increased anxiety, irritability, and, in more serious situations, even seizures.

MEDICATION COMBINATIONS

In the preceding sections we noted that, although some medications do not seem to be helpful when used as the sole medication to treat childhood mood and anxiety disorders, they can be quite beneficial when used in combination with other

medications. Until recently, psychiatrists were wary of prescribing psychotropic medications in combination with each
other and the general practice was to conduct trials of the
most promising drugs in sequential, nonoverlapping fashion.
Thus, if the first drug worked on some symptoms but not
others, or if side effects were problematic, that medication
would be discontinued and a trial with a second medication
would be undertaken, and so on.

Today there is increasing recognition that this approach—
searching for a single medication that will treat the broad
range of symptoms seen in so many depressed youngsters—is
not likely to prove fruitful in most cases. In light of recent
findings that comorbidity tends to be the rule rather than the
exception among depressed youngsters, researchers and clinicians alike have begun to explore the use of judicious combinations of medications targeted to each child's specific constel-
lation of symptoms and problems.

At Yale University, for example, Doctors Davis Gammon
and Tom Brown used a combination of Prozac and Ritalin (a
medication known to be helpful to many children with
ADHD) to treat a group of youngsters with ADHD and mood
disorders. Although these youngsters had not responded to
treatment with Ritalin alone, after eight weeks of combined
treatment, 30 of 32 youngsters in the study showed significant
improvements in mood, attention, behavior, and school performance.[21] There is also some evidence that a combination of
Prozac and a tricyclic antidepressant may be more beneficial
and quicker to take effect than when either medication is used
alone.

BENEFITS OF MEDICATION

When medication is effective, what can we expect to see? As
we noted, people who take antidepressant medication don't
wander about in a slaphappy daze. Confronted with the ups
and downs of daily life, they still feel the normal emotions of

anxiety, annoyance, sadness, and so on. The difference is that these emotions are now less overwhelming and more in proportion to the situation at hand. Among the benefits medication can confer are the following:

- Improved ability to cope: the depressed person is more resilient and better able to "bounce back" from disappointments and setbacks. Concentration, memory, and ability to make decisions are improved, too, so the person can function more effectively and efficiently at school or in the workplace.

- Improved sleep and energy: antidepressants normalize chemical activity in brain systems which control sleep, so they correct sleep problems such as insomnia and interrupted sleep. Unlike conventional "sleeping pills," they induce sleep naturally and are not addictive.

- Appetite regulation: again, antidepressant medications work to restore normal appetite, both in patients who suffer loss of appetite and in those who are driven to eat to excess.

- Decreased irritability, anxiety: when treatment with medication is effective, it's surprising how many of our young patients report that their parents, siblings, teachers, and friends are much easier to get along with. What has happened, of course, is that the depressed youngster is less "prickly" and better able to relate to those around him in a friendly, relaxed fashion. Fears and worries, once all-encompassing, also seem to fade into oblivion when medication takes effect.

Julie, age seventeen, was in her last year of high school when she suffered from a depressive episode so severe that she was only a step away from hospitalization. With prompt intervention, she recovered and was able to return to school for the second semester. Shortly after-

ward, her boyfriend ended their relationship of two years, and friends and family alike feared the worst. Julie, however, handled the situation with remarkable equanimity: after a week or two of tears and moping, she resolutely pulled herself together and began seeing other friends and spending time on her studies.

When her therapist asked how she was managing to cope so well, she grinned and replied, "I guess it must be these miracle drugs!" Then she paused and became serious. "No," she said, "I'm kidding. Sure, I'm sad that Robbie and I broke up and I'm not saying I wouldn't go back to him, given a chance. We've known each other for years and I'm really going to miss him. But talking with you has helped me see that I'm probably going to meet a lot of guys before I find the one that I want to be with for the rest of my life.

"Even so," she added, "I'm really glad that I'm on the medication. If this had happened six months ago, before I went on the medication, I know that I would have gone off the wall. Now I know that I can handle it, even if it's rough. And I think that I can handle other things, too, like when I have a fight with my parents or if one of my friends lets me down. I still don't like it—nobody would—but I don't fall apart and want to kill myself. I just sort of grit my teeth and tell myself that I can deal with it."

In Julie's case, we can see that the medication not only helped her overcome her depression: it also helped her to see that depression did not have to control her life—that she could free herself from its crushing impact. We can see, too, how medication works in combination with psychotherapy to help a depressed youngster "put it all together."

CONCERNS AND QUESTIONS ABOUT MEDICATION

Parents of depressed youngsters are often alarmed when the recommendation is made for a trial of antidepressant medication. The reasons for their concern are many and varied, ranging from an almost instinctive tendency to deny the existence of the problem to a well-reasoned concern about the safety of such medications.

When it comes to medication, young people, too, have questions and objections. While some depressed youngsters are enthusiastic about the possibility that medication will relieve the painful symptoms of depression, others resist taking medication because of the stigma—taking medication means you're "crazy." Others worry that they will lose control, undergo a personality change, and become like robots. They want to know, too, whether antidepressant medication is addictive and whether they can expect to be faced with a lifetime of taking medication.

HOW SAFE ARE THESE MEDICATIONS?

Most parents are appropriately concerned about the safety of all medications, especially for their children. "What are the side effects?" they ask. And "What do we know about long-term use?" Others are concerned about the possibility that their child might become addicted to medication. Still others, having read about specific medications in such sources as the Physicians' Desk Reference[22] (PDR) are reluctant to allow their child to be treated with medications which do not have FDA approval for use in children.

SIDE EFFECTS. Clinicians and researchers agree that, for the most part, children seem to find side effects of psychotropic medications less troublesome than do adults who are treated with the same medications. Annoying side effects can also be minimized by carefully adjusting the medication and monitoring the child's response to it.

As concerns the long-term safety of a particular medication, some of the newer medications simply have not been available long enough for us to be certain of the answer to this question. What we do know, however, is that the long-term effects of untreated depression are usually quite serious. Without treatment, the course of childhood depression tends to be chronic. Each episode of depression increases the likelihood that more episodes will follow and the duration of the episodes increases with subsequent recurrences. It is against this risk that the potential risks and benefits of treatment with antidepressant medication must be weighed.

ADDICTION. The fear that children will become addicted to antidepressants and other psychotropic medications appears to be without foundation. Antidepressants do not create euphoria or "highs," as we discussed above (p. 110), so their potential for addiction is virtually nonexistent. There is also no indication that use of psychotropic medications will lead to substance abuse later on. In fact, since effective treatment of depression and other psychiatric disorders can enable youngsters to think, work, and relate to others more effectively, psychotropic medications may actually be important in **preventing** subsequent problems with substance abuse.

As concerns length of treatment, we usually advise parents and children to simply wait and see how helpful medication is before we address this question. While some young people can discontinue medication after a six- to twelve-month period during which they are symptom-free, others must remain on medication indefinitely. Although we recognize that this can be something of a burden, we liken it to taking care of one's teeth or other personal hygiene needs: it's a nuisance but, if you want to keep your teeth and avoid offending others, you will have to brush and bathe regularly for the rest of your life!

FDA APPROVAL. Parents who read the package inserts

which accompany their child's medication or who turn to the PDR for information about a specific medication are understandably frightened when they read that the medication is "Not approved for use with children below the age of 18" (or 16, or 12, or whatever). Because this is such a common source of confusion, it is imperative that you understand what the term "FDA approved" really means.

The United States Food and Drug Administration (FDA) is a federal agency which was established to protect the public by setting safety standards for foods, cosmetics, and drugs and by regulating the claims manufacturers could make about their products. The process by which a new drug gains FDA approval for the treatment of a specific medical condition is long, arduous, and expensive: it can cost as much as two hundred million dollars to conduct all of the necessary research to prove that the product is both safe and effective.[23]

Unfortunately—but understandably—if a manufacturer believes there is little chance that the investment will pay off in profits, research on the drug's effectiveness with subgroups such as children will not be undertaken. This means that medications which are quite effective for certain conditions may never be labeled by the FDA as suitable for use with these conditions or for certain subgroups who suffer from the conditions. A case in point is that of the drug lithium: although numerous studies supported the efficacy of lithium in the treatment of bipolar disorder, this simple salt could not be patented, so there was no incentive for drug companies to apply for FDA approval. Thus, for many years, manic-depressive patients in the United States were denied the single most effective medication for their painful and disabling condition.

The most important point for you, as a parent, to remember is that FDA guidelines regulate the claims that manufacturers can make for their drugs. They were never intended to govern the way in which physicians prescribe. The FDA explicitly states that these guidelines are in no way meant to limit

medical decision making and that clinical decisions must be
made by physicians and patients in individual situations.

In addition to questions of safety, some parents object to
psychotropic medication on philosophical grounds. These parents often say, "I don't even like to take aspirin when I have a
headache," and they worry that taking medication for a psychiatric condition is just taking the easy way out. "Wouldn't it
be better if he learned to face his problems head on and deal
with them?" they ask. And, "Won't he start to think that he
can't function without medication?"

In response, we point out that depression is not a state of
mind, nor does it indicate a weakness in character or will.
Depression is an illness that is as "real" as diabetes so we ask,
"If your child were diabetic, would you deny him insulin on
the grounds that he should just 'tough it out'?"

Our reply to the second question—"Won't children think
that they can't function without medication?"—is a resound-
ing "NO!" Many adolescents perceive medication as a "cop-
out" and an indication that they can't cope as well as their
peers. As clinicians, we find that the problem is seldom one of
convincing a youngster that he can function without medication: instead, we often talk ourselves breathless to persuade
our depressed adolescents that they do, indeed, need to take
medication in order to function at optimal levels.

MISINFORMATION

As we noted in a preceding section, people have been exposed
to all sorts of myths and misinformation about medications
used to treat psychiatric disorders. High on this list are the
drugs Prozac and Ritalin, both of which have been subjected
to undeserved unfavorable publicity.

But not all misinformation and misunderstandings about

psychotropic medications can be blamed on supermarket tab-
loids and sensationalistic television programs. Sadly, in their
search for information about these medications, some parents
turn to sources such as the Physicians' Desk Reference and,
misinterpreting both the purpose of the PDR and the information it contains, manage to scare themselves away from medications which might be of great benefit to their children.

We certainly applaud the desire of parents to be well informed about their child's treatment—that's why we have
written this book! However, we do not think that information
in the PDR or similar sources is likely to be very helpful to
parents of depressed youngsters. In addition to confusion associated with the term "FDA approved" noted on p. 115,
there is also the fact that parents may become unduly alarmed
about side effects which are extremely rare but which manufacturers are nonetheless required to list. Dosage information
is also likely to be misleading as far as child and adolescent
patients are concerned. Contrary to the popular belief that,
since children are physically smaller than adults, they require
smaller doses of medications, the way in which children me-
tabolize medication often requires that **larger**, not smaller,
doses be used for maximum benefit.

In summary we believe that, when medication is concerned, there is no substitute for competent professional advice. If you suspect that the professional working with your
child lacks specific expertise with psychotropic medications,
get a second opinion from someone known to be skilled in this
area. As we noted earlier, university medical centers are usu
ally a good place to begin, especially if research involving the
use of medication with depressed children and adolescents is
under way at a university near you.

Parent support groups which recognize the role of disordered brain chemistry in childhood psychiatric conditions can
also be a source of information. One such group is the National Alliance for the Mentally Ill Children and Adolescents
(NAMI-CAN), a support group for parents of children with

neurobiological disorders such as depression (see Chapter 10 for more information). Although this group cannot make recommendations concerning specific mental health professionals, they can provide information about support groups in your area. By attending meetings, you can network with other parents and obtain the names of professionals who have helped children whose problems are similar to those of your child.

WHO SHOULD PRESCRIBE MEDICATION?

Research and clinical experience have shown that antidepressant medications are safe when they are prescribed and closely monitored by a trained professional with expertise in the area of psychopharmacology. While there are certainly exceptions, such expertise is found only among **child psychiatrists.** You probably have only the haziest notion of what a child psychiatrist does or what the training entails, but as a parent, you should know that child psychiatrists must complete medical school, a one-year internship, a two-year residency in general psychiatry, and a two-year fellowship in child psychiatry.

When we look at the years of study and training involved in becoming a child psychiatrist, we can see that it is no wonder that child psychiatrists are literally very few and far between. In addition, some parents fear that their child will be stigmatized by entering treatment with a child psychiatrist. For these reasons, parents often ask whether another physician, such as a pediatrician, a family practice physician, or a pediatric neurologist, can prescribe psychotropic medications. By law, of course, any licensed physician can prescribe these drugs. However, success with these medications requires a great deal of experience with large numbers of patients. Unless the prescribing professional has such experience, the youngster's response to treatment is likely to be poor.

If a child psychiatrist is not available in your community, you should certainly consider obtaining the services of one in the nearest metropolitan area. In some cases, once a youngster has been stabilized on an effective medication regimen, a local physician can monitor the child, so that follow-up appointments with the child psychiatrist are needed only every six months or so.

ALTERNATIVE INTERVENTIONS

In addition to medication, other methods are available to combat depression in children and adolescents. For the most part, methods such as electroconvulsive therapy (ECT) are not in widespread use today, except under restricted circumstances. Nevertheless, since ECT does have a place in the treatment of some seriously depressed youngsters who do not respond to other forms of treatment, we will briefly review it in the following section.

ECT

The idea of producing convulsions (seizures) to treat severe mood disorders grew out of the observation that some patients who suffered from both epilepsy and depression showed dramatic improvement in psychiatric symptoms after a seizure. Acting on this observation, doctors used large doses of insulin to produce seizures in seriously depressed patients and found that many improved remarkably. The use of insulin to produce seizures is not without danger, however, so insulin was soon replaced by the much safer method of producing a seizure by passing an electrical current across small electrodes placed on the skull.

While ECT sounds frightening—even barbaric—it is actually a safe, painless procedure. Patients are comfortably sedated during the procedure and closely monitored throughout. ECT is usually administered two or three times a week, for a total of six to twelve treatments.

THE PROS AND CONS. Short-term side effects of ECT include confusion, disorientation, anxiety, and memory disturbances. Although these problems usually clear up within a few hours or days following treatment, some mild memory impairment might persist for up to a couple of months. Research using computed axial tomography (CAT) and magnetic resonance imaging (MRI) does **not** suggest a link between ECT and brain damage.[24]

Obviously, ECT is not an appropriate treatment for most depressed youngsters. However, based on the limited research available, it can be very helpful—even life-saving—for severely depressed or bipolar youths who have not responded to any other form of treatment.[25]

LIGHT THERAPY

Treatment with bright artificial light has been found to be helpful for children and adults who suffer from the cyclical mood disorder known as Seasonal Affective Disorder, or SAD. As we discussed in Chapter 1, people who suffer from SAD have annually recurring episodes of depression. These episodes, which usually have their onset in the autumn and resolve in the spring, are characterized by low energy, irritability, and excessive sleeping and eating.

In the early 1980s, researchers at the National Institute of Mental Health in Bethesda, Maryland, discovered that many people afflicted with SAD respond to treatment with bright artificial light. Using specially designed "light boxes" which deliver as much as 10,000 lux (an amount which is more than twenty times the amount of light in the average living room but less than the amount to which one is exposed on a bright spring day), they have amassed very convincing evidence that people who suffer from seasonal mood disorders can be helped with light treatment.[26]

Treatment involves spending as little as thirty minutes a day in close proximity to a light box and the results, which include improved mood, energy, and concentration, can often be observed within a few days. Children as well as adults have been shown to benefit from this simple but effective treatment.[27]

THE PROS AND CONS. Light therapy is a simple, noninvasive treatment with no known side effects. However, it should not be undertaken without the benefit of professional supervision. Before you consider light therapy for your child, you will want to obtain more information about SAD and light therapy, as well as the names of knowledgeable and experienced professionals across the country who can supervise your child's treatment.*

---

* For information about SAD, the benefits of light therapy, and the names of knowledgeable professionals in your area, contact The Sun Box Company, 19217 Orbit Drive, Gaithersburg, MD 20879 or call them at 1-800-LITE-YOU.

SEVEN

What Should We Do in a Crisis?

Suicidal Behavior and Psychiatric Hospitalization

SUICIDE: A PARENT'S WORST FEAR

OF ALL THE PAINFUL EXPERIENCES that can befall a human being, the death of one's child is surely one of the most tragic. For those left behind, the loss is even more devastating when the child's death is self-inflicted.

In recent years the popular press has directed a spotlight on teenage suicide. Although it is media hyperbole to describe suicide as "epidemic" among adolescents, the statistics themselves are actually quite alarming. Suicide is now a leading cause of death among adolescents[1] and some studies find that as many as 11 percent of all high school students admit to having made at least one suicide attempt.[2] As if this weren't frightening enough, we are confronted with the fact that suicide rates, like rates of depression, are increasing in the population, especially among young people.

Suicide is rare in children below the age of ten, but it is by no means impossible. Children as young as preschoolers can have suicidal thoughts and ideas and some even attempt to act on these thoughts and wishes by throwing themselves in front of a car, jumping out of a window, or deliberately engaging in other high-risk activities.

When the parish priest informed them that their son had told him of a plan to kill himself, Chad's parents were stunned and disbelieving. At age nine, Chad seemed to have the world by the proverbial tail. A bright, athletic youngster with a droll sense of humor, he earned good grades in private school, where he was a great favorite among students and teachers alike.

In spite of these accomplishments, Chad clearly suffered from serious depression. In an interview with a clinical psychologist, he talked openly about his difficulties, stating that he had been very anxious and unhappy for at least three years. Of his reputation as a joker and class clown, he said, "People think I'm a happy kid; they don't know that I'm unhappy a lot." He acknowledged that he wanted to die "because I have so many problems in my life." Among the problems, he listed squabbles with his siblings, difficulty controlling his temper, and the fact that he found schoolwork taxing and difficult and was afraid that he would fail. In a matter-of-fact fashion, Chad described his plan to kill himself by driving a car off a cliff across the street, adding that he would take the older of the family's two cars "because my parents want to get rid of it anyway."

With the onset of adolescence, suicidal behavior increases steadily. Although girls outnumber boys in suicide attempts, especially after the age of fourteen or so, boys outnumber girls in terms of those who actually die as a result of their own efforts. Among young people who commit suicide, the most common method is with firearms, followed by hanging and jumping from a height. While drug overdose is the most common method in suicide **attempts,** it actually accounts for few completed suicides.[3]

It is not surprising that the rates of suicide are increasing at rates which parallel those of depression, since the relationship between depression and suicide is a close one. Adults who suffer from depressive illness are **thirty times** more likely than others in the population to commit suicide.[4]

In young people, too, the link between depression and suicidal behavior is close. Certainly not all depressed youths kill themselves or even attempt to do so but depression constitutes the single greatest risk factor for suicide. For example, depressed teenage girls are **twenty-three times** more likely to attempt suicide than other girls their age who are not depressed.

What other factors increase the likelihood that a young person will engage in some form of suicidal behavior? We know that the risk of suicide is increased when any of the following complications are present or have occurred in a teenager's past:

- **Previous suicide attempt:** Any young person who has engaged in suicidal behavior in the past should be considered at particular risk to repeat the behavior. Despite the popular view of adolescence as a time of great emotional upheaval, suicidal acts fall outside the range of behavior we consider developmentally normal and, when they occur, they almost always indicate significant emotional problems. Even if a youngster has only made what we would call a "gesture," the behavior should still be taken quite seriously: since teenagers are surprisingly poor judges of what might actually be lethal, the next such "gesture" could well prove fatal.

- **Substance abuse:** The use of alcohol and drugs can contribute to suicidal behavior in a number of ways. Not only do drugs and alcohol impair judgment; they also lower inhibitions and increase the likelihood of impulsive behavior. Alcohol, in particular, tends to exaggerate feelings of depression and anger, making it more likely that a youngster beset with problems will decide that death offers the only relief from intense psychological pain. In fact, many adolescent suicide victims have been found to be intoxicated at the time of their deaths.

· Coexisting psychiatric conditions: Teenagers who engage in antisocial behavior such as fighting, stealing, and running away from home are also likely to abuse drugs and alcohol. It makes sense, then, that young people who are conduct-disordered are at a greater risk for suicidal behavior.

Another psychiatric disorder which increases the risk of suicide is a condition called Borderline Personality Disorder. This condition is characterized by very intense but unstable relationships with others, rapid mood changes, and problems controlling inappropriate and intense anger. People who are diagnosed with Borderline Personality Disorder can't stand to be alone and often have chronic feelings of emptiness or boredom. They tend to be impulsive and to engage in potentially dangerous behavior, such as reckless driving, spending sprees, casual sex, substance abuse, and shoplifting. A substantial number of depressed adolescents exhibit these kinds of symptoms during the period when they are depressed[5] and, for obvious reasons, they are at greatly increased risk for suicide.

· Family dysfunction: In families of suicidal adolescents it is not uncommon to find that other family members also suffer from psychiatric disorders and there is often a great deal of conflict among family members. In fact, many of these families are best described as multiple-problem families in which the parents are distant, preoccupied with their own problems, and emotionally unavailable to their children. These families appear to have poor communication and problem-solving skills and family interaction often involves power struggles.[6]

Although, in the past, research tended to highlight psychiatric problems in the mothers of suicidal youngsters, more recent research has shown that fathers also play a significant role; specifically, fathers of suicidal adolescents are themselves often depressed, uncommunicative, and cut off from their wives and children.[7]

It is difficult to separate the contribution made by genetics from that which is due to the pain and stress caused by ongoing problems within the family. Again, it is likely that both factors play a part.

• **Family history of suicide:** Like depression, suicide "runs in families." A youngster is more likely to engage in suicidal behavior if one or more of his relatives committed suicide, especially if that relative was a parent. Again, the question of nature or nurture—heredity or environment—comes up and, once again, we find that the answer includes "a little of both." Certainly loss of a parent through suicide is a traumatic experience which could well result in a young person becoming depressed and, ultimately, suicidal. Some social scientists have also advanced the notion that, if a parent or other relative commits suicide, the taboo against suicide is reduced in the mind of the young person, so suicide is not seen as such an impossible or reprehensible act.

However, heredity appears to make a contribution too: just as there seems to be a genetic factor involved in depression, genes also appear to play a role in vulnerability to suicidal behavior. As a group, suicidal people have abnormalities in the way in which their brains manufacture and use serotonin, an important neurotransmitter in the central nervous system. Low levels of 5-HIAA, a chemical substance which results from the breakdown of serotonin, have been found in the spinal fluid of many people who have made suicide attempts, especially ones in which the method has been violent in nature.[8] Neuroscientists have recently located a specific gene which plays a principal role in this process, thereby identifying at least one way in which a tendency to commit suicide can actually be passed along from generation to generation.[9]

- **Poor social skills, few friends:** More than any other period in the human lifespan, adolescence is a time when relationships with peers assume an all-encompassing importance. Peer relationships—or the lack thereof—play an important role in adolescent depression and suicide. A network of caring friends can certainly act as a buffer against the negative effects of living in a poorly functioning family but, when we look at the friends of suicidal adolescents, we find that they, too, tend to have personal and family problems. This means that they can't always be counted on to provide stability and support to a desperate youngster. In other cases, we find that depressed youngsters withdraw socially so they lose whatever support their friends might otherwise offer. Finally, as we noted earlier, since depressed youngsters often have poor social skills, they may have few friends and thus be in no position to derive support from their peers.

- **Stressful life events:** Young people who attempt suicide often have backgrounds which include painful and frightening events such as physical abuse or the loss of a parent through death or divorce. Increasingly, too, we see media reports of cases in which a young person specifically cites sexual abuse as the reason for suicidal behavior.

Among the most overlooked sources of stress associated with adolescent suicide are the social stigma and isolation suffered by those who are in a sexual minority; that is, those who are lesbian, gay, or bisexual. Of known adolescent suicides, 30 percent—almost one third!—are of sexual minority youths, and suicide attempts are two to three times more frequent in this group than among heterosexual teenagers.[10]

PRECIPITANTS

We have outlined several background factors which indicate that a young person is at an increased risk for suicide. But what is it that sets the match to the dry tinder? What happens to push a predisposed youngster over the edge? When we look at youths who have attempted or completed suicide, we find that some events are particularly likely to trigger suicidal behavior in vulnerable youths.

Since adolescents are extremely self-conscious, we might anticipate that these triggers would involve situations which leave the young person feeling rejected, abandoned, angry, and humiliated. Breaking up with a boyfriend or a girlfriend is a situation which immediately comes to mind in this context. While adults may characterize these usually short-lived liaisons as "puppy love" and look upon them with tolerance and mild amusement, adolescents tend to take their intimate relationships very seriously indeed. A quarrel which might seem minor in the eyes of an adult can seem like the end of the world to a sensitive teenager, especially if the teenager also suffers from depression.

Diagnosed at an early age with Attention-Deficit Disorder and learning disabilities, sixteen-year-old Lisa struggled for years to keep up with her peers. When she was eight, her parents divorced after years of conflict. The divorce proceedings were bitter and Lisa was the victim of a protracted custody battle. With tutoring, Lisa managed to keep up with her classmates in elementary school but she floundered badly when she entered high school.

A relationship with a supportive boyfriend boosted her self-esteem and her social standing. Since they studied together and since the boyfriend himself was a good student, Lisa's grades even improved. Reluctant at first, Lisa eventually agreed to sexual intimacy, although this went against her religious principles. All went well for several months, until the boyfriend's interest began to wane and he became increasingly unavailable. When she learned that he had invited another girl to his senior prom, she impulsively raided her father's medicine chest and, after ingesting a variety of pills, was taken by ambulance to a local emergency room.

As any parent of a teenager can attest, adolescents are exquisitely sensitive to perceived humiliation and loss of face. It's not surprising, then, that another trigger for suicidal behavior involves disputes with parents in which the young person emerges feeling degraded and in a one-down position. Other situations which place a youngster in a vulnerable position are those in which the youngster faces disciplinary action in school or through the legal system.

When any of these factors is involved, the effect is almost immediate: young people who engage in suicidal behavior for any of these reasons often do so within twenty-four hours of the precipitating event.[11]

Another factor which can serve as a trigger for suicide in some vulnerable young people is publicity about other teenagers who have committed suicide. There have been several well-documented reports of suicides occurring in "clusters"; that is, adolescents become suicidal themselves after the suicide of a friend or schoolmate. In one Pittsburgh high school, for example, the self-inflicted firearm death of a former student was followed in rapid succession by the suicide of two students and suicide attempts or gestures in three others.[12]

Even publicity about a teenage suicide victim in another town or state can precipitate suicidal behavior in susceptible

young people. The media—television, in particular—have
been accused of fueling what they have termed an "epidemic"
of teenage suicide and, in fact, there is evidence that supports
this accusation. We know, for example, that the suicide rate
among young people increases by as much as 10 percent in the
one- to two-week period immediately following media publicity about teenage suicide. This effect holds whether the publicity consists of headlines or news reports of an actual suicide,
or a fictional account, such as a television movie.[13]

How can we account for this "contagion effect"? In the
case of youngsters who attempt suicide following the self-
inflicted death of a friend, the suicidal behavior may be the
result of grief and depression over the loss, especially if the
friendship was close.[14] (Remember that disturbed youngsters
tend to associate with and befriend one another, so those who
are most likely to be emotionally affected by the loss of a peer
through suicide are usually those who, themselves, have few
resources upon which to rely in a crisis.)

It is much more difficult to account for the increase in the
rate of youth suicide that follows on the heels of publicity
about an unknown youngster who decides to take his own life.
Again, we are left with the explanation that bearing witness to
another's suicide, even at a distance, somehow lessens the taboo against suicide and makes it seem more like an acceptable
option.

In summary, what can we say about young people who
are most likely to engage in suicidal behavior? We know that
depressed youngsters are clearly at greater risk for suicide,
especially if they are impulsive and frequently violate family
and social rules. A history of previous suicide attempts, a family history which includes suicide, and use of drugs and alcohol are particularly significant risk factors. The more isolated
the youngster and the fewer the supportive friends and family
members around him, the greater the risk that a despondent
young person will choose suicide as an option.

INTERVENTION: PREVENTING A TRAGEDY

If your teenager fits a high-risk profile, you shouldn't panic but you certainly should be aware of the risks that additional stressors can pose to a vulnerable youngster. You can't hope to avoid these stressors—you can't, for example, prevent a disenchanted boyfriend or girlfriend from ending a relationship, nor can you stop an impulsive youngster from running afoul of rules in school, at home, or in society at large and then having to face the consequences. However, you can be alert to such problems when they come up and you can make yourself available to help the youngster talk about and begin to work through the problem.

There are also some red flags that should warn you of impending danger. If your child begins to give away treasured possessions or if he or she suddenly seems to be trying to make amends for past wrongs, be particularly alert to the possibility of suicide. If a youngster actually talks about taking his life, especially if he has a well-thought out plan to do so, it is time for parents to take immediate action. What should you do?

- **Keep the lines of communication open.** Confronted with a loved one who is contemplating suicide, the average person is understandably at a loss as to how to react. Probably the most common response is to minimize or deny the problem—in effect, to try to make it go away by pretending that it doesn't exist. But sweeping it under the rug won't work: responses such as "You know you don't mean that," or "Come on, things aren't that bad" don't really change the way the suicidal person feels—but they do make it less likely that he will continue to confide in you.

  Instead of arguing or jumping in with reassurance, concentrate all of your efforts on listening closely and carefully to what your child has to say. Don't be afraid that talking candidly will put ideas in his head; those ideas are already there. By bringing these ideas out and discussing them in a reasonably calm manner, you will have taken the first step: you will have removed the burden of secrecy from a youngster who is already sufficiently burdened.

· **Provide support and set limits.** Be quite direct with your child in assuring him of your love for him and your concern for his safety. Be clear, too, in conveying the message that suicide is taboo in your family. At first blush, this might seem rather silly but, as psychologists Gerald Oster and Janice Caro[15] have found in their work with depressed and suicidal adolescents, some parents cannot give their teenagers a strong message against suicidal behavior. This is not a time for ambivalence or for beating around the bush. The statement should be clear: "Suicide is against the rules in our family. We will help you work out these problems so that you don't feel so desperate but killing yourself is not an option, no matter what."

   You must also obtain a commitment from the youngster that he will not attempt to hurt himself and that, if he does have suicidal thoughts and feelings, he should tell you before he initiates any action.

· **Ensure the child's safety.** Even though you have obtained your child's agreement that he will not pursue a suicidal course, you must take additional steps to protect him from his own impulsiveness. Let your child know that you will assume responsibility for keeping him safe until the crisis has passed. Then act on this assurance by limiting access to potentially lethal methods. If there is a gun in your home, get rid of it immediately. Check all medicine cabinets carefully. Remove all medications, including such seemingly innocuous drugs as aspirin, and place them under lock and key. (You might protest that someone who is determined to commit suicide will simply find another way. But remember that youth suicide is usually an impulsive act and, by making it more difficult to carry out a spur-of-the-moment plan, you could prevent a tragedy.)

Don't attempt to hide these precautions from the young person. The message you send by this behavior is not "I don't trust you," but "I care enough about you to want to keep you safe." In the same vein, be straight forward in letting the youngster know that, for his safety, you will monitor him quite closely until all can agree that such monitoring is no longer necessary.

- **Get professional help immediately.** If your child is currently in therapy, call the therapist to discuss the problem. If the child is not in therapy, make arrangements to have a professional evaluation immediately—certainly by the next day—and keep the youngster under surveillance in the interim. The result of the evaluation may be the recommendation to hospitalize the youngster. If that is the case, what should you do?

PSYCHIATRIC HOSPITALIZATION AND INPATIENT TREATMENT

WHEN SHOULD A CHILD BE HOSPITALIZED?

The decision to admit a child or teenager to a psychiatric hospital is a complicated one because it depends on so many factors. In general, however, we think that hospitalization is indicated when any or all of the following conditions exist:

- If the youngster is a danger to himself or others, hospitalization is certainly indicated. Youngsters considered to be a danger to themselves or others are those who are actively suicidal and/or assaultive. If a youngster has made a suicide attempt, or if he has a clear plan to carry out such an attempt, hospitalization is probably necessary. Similarly, if a youngster has assaulted people around him with intent to do actual harm, or if he has a plan to inflict serious harm on another person, hospitalization is in order to prevent the possibility of a tragedy.

• If a child's behavior is extremely dysfunctional, hospitalization should certainly be considered. Children who literally cannot get out of bed in the morning; who prowl the house at odd hours because they cannot sleep; who burst into uncontrollable tears or tantrums without provocation; who abuse drugs and alcohol— these are all youngsters who need immediate professional attention, perhaps in an inpatient setting. Hospitalization is also advisable if the youngster seems to be losing contact with reality; if he engages in bizarre behavior, for example, or if he is hallucinating or experiencing delusions.

• If parents and others in the youngster's immediate environment cannot meet the child's need for security and containment, hospitalization must be seriously considered. In some families, the parents may be so overwhelmed by the child's problems and so exhausted from struggling with practical matters like work and child care that they are simply unable to provide a secure environment for the child during a crisis.

As a parent, you must examine and weigh all of the pros and cons before making such an important decision. One of your principal worries is likely to be the stigma your child will face as a result of having been a "mental patient." This is not a trivial concern, since our society has not yet fully recognized that illnesses like depression are every bit as real as a broken bone or an attack of appendicitis.

In this regard, the good news is that your child's peers

and teachers are more likely to respond with sympathy than with rejection when they learn of the youngster's problems. The bad news is that you, as parents, can expect to face more censure from your peers than your child will from his. Those closest to you, including your coworkers, your neighbors, and your immediate family, may convey their disapproval in ways which range from the subtle to the very blatant. Saddest of all is the fact that the very people from whom you would most expect help may be the least likely to offer the kind of assistance you really need. Because older people are less knowledgeable about psychiatric problems, you might find that your parents, in particular, are so upset and distraught by the situation that they can offer you no support. Therefore, you must put your own feelings aside before you can act in your child's best interests.

You must also be prepared to deal with your child's reaction to impending hospitalization. Some young people respond with intense anger and threats to run away or kill themselves. Others use guilt trips to try to dissuade their parents from moving ahead with plans to place them in a hospital. Some, however, accept and agree to hospitalization as the best course of action. In our clinical experience, this is most likely to happen when the recommendation for hospitalization comes from, or is at least supported by, a therapist with whom the youngster has developed a trusting relationship. It is particularly helpful if the therapist actually knows some of the hospital staff and is familiar with the program.

WHAT CAN HOSPITALIZATION OFFER?

Once you've dealt with these hurdles—and they are big ones indeed—you will be more prepared to deal with some of the practical issues involved in hospitalization. You can then ask, "What advantages does inpatient care offer my child over those of outpatient treatment right now?" The paramount question concerns safety: if you are not confident that you can

assure the safety of your child during the crisis period, don't
be afraid to admit it. As with other serious ailments, hospitals
are specifically designed to handle life-threatening illnesses, so
there is no shame in acknowledging that they can do the job
better than you can.

What other advantages can hospitalization offer a youngster who suffers from depression?

- **Comprehensive assessment.** When a young person is
  admitted to a psychiatric hospital, the first order of
  business is usually a comprehensive series of medical
  and psychological tests. Typically, this includes a complete physical and neurological examination as well as
  laboratory studies of blood and urine. These tests are
  administered to rule out the possibility that a physical
  illness such as a thyroid condition is a contributing factor in the youngster's difficulties. An electrocardiogram
  (EKG) is often done to rule out any heart problems that
  might make the use of certain medications risky. If
  there is reason to suspect a seizure disorder (epilepsy)
  or a progressive disease of the central nervous system,
  additional tests would be performed, such as an electroencephalogram (EEG), computerized axial tomography
  (CAT scan), or magnetic resonance imaging (MRI).

  Psychological tests usually include intelligence
  tests, personality tests, and academic achievement tests
  to evaluate current level of intellectual, emotional, and
  academic functioning. A speech and language evaluation is often included, since so many youngsters who
  suffer from psychiatric disorders also have undiagnosed
  developmental language problems which hinder their
  ability to express themselves and understand others.

  All of these tests are certainly available outside of
  an inpatient setting and, in fact, many of them are
  likely to have been performed already if the youngster
  was in psychiatric treatment before being hospitalized.

The advantage offered by the hospital, however, is "one-stop shopping," since all services are available under one roof. This not only expedites what would otherwise be a long and arduous process; it has the additional advantage that the specialists themselves are available to confer with one another to puzzle out complicated cases.

- **Stabilization of the child and the family.** Intensive treatment of the adolescent helps stabilize the youngster quickly, bringing to a halt a downward spiral and making it possible for him to then receive treatment in a less controlling and restricted environment. Just the enforced routine of the hospital—meals at certain times, a set bedtime—can work wonders with a youngster whose illness has resulted in a topsy-turvy world of lost sleep and poor nutrition.

  At the same time, intensive work with the family helps the family identify unsatisfactory patterns of behavior, mobilize resources, and begin to work together to help the troubled youngster. In the safety of the hospital setting, the youngster and the family have an opportunity to try out new, more adaptive behaviors and coping skills and to receive on-the-spot feedback and coaching from professionals.

- **Close monitoring and careful observation.** With a team of professionals available around the clock, the child's safety is assured in the event of impulsive or self-destructive behavior. In addition, with such close observation, the hospital affords an ideal opportunity to assess the way in which a young person copes with problems, both as an individual and as a member of a family unit. Also, since many teenage patients are hospitalized at least in part because of drug and alcohol abuse, the hospital setting lets professionals see how the youngster functions after a period of enforced abstinence. Finally, many young patients who are admitted to the hospital are already on various kinds of antidepressant medication but the medications have not proved sufficiently helpful. Hospitalization allows the doctors to gradually withdraw medication, observe how the youngster functions without it, and to evaluate the effectiveness of new medications.

SELECTING A HOSPITAL

Very few of us would know how to go about evaluating a psychiatric facility, let alone be able to undertake such an endeavor in the midst of the stress and turmoil that usually surround the decision to hospitalize a child for psychiatric reasons. There are, however, a few simple guidelines offered by the American Academy of Child and Adolescent Psychiatry[16] which can help you make a wise choice.

First and foremost, the hospital should be approved by the Joint Commission for the Accreditation of Healthcare Organizations (JCAHO), an organization which sets standards of care for hospitals. This means that the facility has met the JCAHO's criteria for inpatient psychiatric treatment programs for children and adolescents. One such criterion, for example, is that children under sixteen should be admitted only to programs that are designed for children and adolescents and are physically distinct from programs for adult psychiatric patients. Adolescents sixteen and older may be admitted to adult units but should be treated in a program specifically designed for adolescent psychiatric patients.

The Academy also recommends that the treatment program should be under the direction of a fully trained child and adolescent psychiatrist, if the patient is younger than fourteen years of age. Children fourteen and older may be treated by a general psychiatrist who has had specialized training and supervised experience in working with adolescents. The decision to admit a young person to the facility should be made (or at least confirmed within twenty-four hours) by such a qualified psychiatrist, who will evaluate the patient and determine whether less restrictive treatment settings, such as outpatient care, might be more appropriate.

WHAT CAN YOU EXPECT "ON THE INSIDE"?

In the minds of many people, a psychiatric hospital is at best one step removed from prison. Old stereotypes of the mental institution as a snake pit come up, calling forth images of pitiful souls living in filthy, degrading conditions and tormented by the likes of Nurse Ratchet, the infamous head nurse in *One Flew Over the Cuckoo's Nest*. While there might have been some truth to this picture many years ago, things are quite different today. To be sure, the proliferation of private, for-profit psychiatric hospitals spawned some abuses (for example, there have been cases in which hospitals have been accused of virtually kidnapping troubled youngsters in order to keep the vacancy rate low and the profits high). Such abuses are increasingly rare, however, and the upside is that these facilities offer a setting in which most of us would not be afraid to place our children.

In general, you can expect that the physical plant and facilities will be at least moderately pleasant, with up-to-date amenities. Common areas like the lounge and the dining room are usually bright, cheerful places with comfortable furniture. Bear in mind, however, that any place in which a group of youngsters is housed is bound to show some signs of wear and tear, no matter how much effort is expended on upkeep. Sleeping accommodations are usually such that a youngster will have at least one roommate, so you cannot expect that your child will have his own room. There will be security features, too, like locked elevators and barred windows, that will be disturbing to you.

There will also be the other patients, the people with whom your child will be living and interacting during his stay

in the hospital. What will they be like? In all candor, you are
not likely to find a group of wholesome, corn-fed youngsters
who could model for a Boy Scout advertisement. In fact, you
will probably be dismayed to find that many of the other patients bear a striking resemblance to your child's most objectionable friends—the ones you would most prefer to have
move to another state or maybe another planet.

You will probably have concerns about how long your
child will be hospitalized. Your fear is that, once he is admitted, you will forfeit all control and may never be able to re-
trieve him. As your child's legal guardian, you have the right
to remove him from the hospital even if the doctors don't
agree with your decision. It's true that, in the past, when a
child entered a psychiatric facility it was usually for a long
period of time—months, at least, and often years. Obviously
such care was quite expensive. Economic conditions today dic-
tate that all hospital stays be quite brief, so the average length
of stay in a psychiatric hospital is now only about a month.[17]
Mental health professionals in inpatient settings have learned
to move swiftly and efficiently to diagnose problems and to
formulate treatment goals that can be accomplished in the limited time available.

TREATMENT PROGRAMS IN THE HOSPITAL

After assessment procedures have been completed, the team of
professionals assigned to work with your child during his hospital stay will meet to discuss the results and to develop a
treatment plan. The treatment plan should be quite specific in
terms of goals and objectives that will be achieved during the
hospital stay: for example, one goal might be to eliminate suicidal impulses so that, by the time he is discharged, the young
person will no longer have active suicidal thoughts and will
know what to do if he feels suicidal in the future. Other likely
objectives might include alleviating the depressed mood and
improving communication in the youngster's family.

The treatment plan should also outline what kinds of treatment methods will be used in the hospital to accomplish the goals. The psychiatric hospital is ideally equipped to offer a variety of treatment methods, some of which are available only in a hospital setting. An example of this is what is called "milieu therapy"; that is, in addition to the formally structured parts of the treatment program, the time that the youngster spends interacting with the other patients and the staff is incorporated into the patient's treatment in specific ways. For example, a socially withdrawn youngster can be encouraged and assisted to interact with others, while an impulsive, aggressive youngster can be helped on the spot with problems of temper control.

More structured methods of treatment used in the hospital will include individual psychotherapy with a member of the treatment team. Group psychotherapy is also used to help youngsters learn about themselves and their problems as they work with others who are grappling with similar difficulties. Since peer relationships are so important to adolescents, teenagers can derive particular benefit from peer feedback and interaction.

In recent years family therapy has become an increasingly important part of the hospital treatment of depressed youngsters. In fact, research and clinical experience indicate that parent and family involvement is critical if treatment is to succeed. In one study, for example, treatment of adolescent patients resulted in a 64 percent success rate when parents were involved, whereas failure of parents to participate led to treatment failure in almost 100 percent of the cases.[18] In some hospitals family therapy and group therapy are combined into a unique form of treatment known as multiple family groups. According to proponents of this approach, adolescents are less resistant to feedback from parents of their peers than from their own parents, while parents, in turn, are more receptive to criticism when it comes from someone else's child.

Other forms of treatment available in the hospital include art therapy, music therapy, and occupational therapy. These activities allow depressed youngsters to express and grapple with their feelings through avenues other than language.

WHAT'S NEXT? PLANNING FOR DISCHARGE

Before your child leaves the hospital, there will be what is usually called a "discharge conference." At this meeting, members of the child's treatment team meet with the family to provide a summary report of what has taken place during the hospital stay and to finalize plans for care and follow-up when the child leaves the hospital. Recommendations which emerge from this conference should be quite specific and should include such things as where and with whom the child will live; what mental health services he will receive and from whom; and what school he will attend and what special services should be provided in the school setting.[19]

It is particularly important to plan for continuity of care, so that the youngster's treatment can proceed smoothly and without interruption after he is discharged from the hospital. One of the best ways in which to promote continuity of care is to invite the youngster's outpatient therapist to attend the discharge conference. Attendance at this meeting provides the outpatient therapist with a great deal of information about the youngster's progress, as well an opportunity to discuss specific aspects of care with a team of other professionals.

Not all youngsters who have completed a hospital stay will be discharged directly back into outpatient care. Some might require additional time in a structured setting and, as an intermediate step, will be placed in a day-hospital program. Youngsters who are enrolled in such programs live at home but spend most of their waking hours in a facility which offers intensive involvement in the kind of treatment program found in an inpatient facility. When the youngster is ready for discharge from this facility, a discharge conference should be held and the professional who will serve as the child's outpatient therapist should be in attendance.

EIGHT

How Can the Family Help?

Daily Life with the Depressed Youngster

THE PROBLEMS PARENTS FACE

IF YOUR CHILD SUFFERS from depression—whether of long duration or sudden onset—it's a safe bet that in your search for help you've read all kinds of books on child rearing. It's also a safe bet that you've been confused by what you've read, since every so-called "expert" claims to have access to revealed truth, but no two experts seem to agree on much of anything.

All theories and advice aside, however, there is one point on which we can all agree: parenting is a supremely challenging experience. Only on old-fashioned television sitcoms are the children always happy and well adjusted. In real life—yours and mine—even the most delightful children can sometimes be demanding and exasperating beyond all tolerance. In real life, too, most parents bear very little resemblance to June

Cleaver, that relentlessly cheerful paragon of maternal virtue
in the 1950s TV classic "Leave It to Beaver."

As difficult as it is to be a parent, how much more difficult it is to be the parent of a child or adolescent who suffers
from a mood disorder! This is especially true if, as is often the
case, the depressed youngster also has a coexisting condition
such as Attention Deficit Disorder or Oppositional Defiant
Disorder. These children give new meaning to the word "maddening" when their squabbles with siblings go on from morning till night and when every other utterance is a complaint or
an "I hate you." Maddening, too, is their utter inability to see
how their own behavior contributes to their difficulties: no
matter what the situation, others are always to blame for the
problem. When called to account for misbehavior, their stock
response is "It's not fair—you always blame me."

Perhaps the ultimate in maddening occurs when, after a
special event or a pleasant family outing, the child ends the
day by picking a fight or by throwing a world-class tantrum.
"Auggh!" you shriek silently—or maybe out loud. "Won't
anything ever make this child happy?"

Parents of depressed youngsters face other problems as
well. They face **shame and embarrassment** when their child's
extreme separation anxiety results in wild shrieks and tearful
scenes at the door of the preschool or day care facility. It's
humiliating, too, when an angry, depressed youngster throws
a full-blown tantrum in front of his shocked grandparents or
when the behavior of an out-of-control adolescent results in
police being called to the scene while all the neighbors look
on.

There are **confusion and bewilderment** when you consult
ten people and get ten different kinds of advice.

> *"When he was a toddler, his pediatrician told me it
> was just the 'terrible twos' and that he would outgrow it.
> My mother-in-law thinks we spoil him and that all he
> needs is a good spanking. But my mother says we should*

back off and give him a little space. We had a conference with his teachers because his grades have hit rock bottom; they told us he's lazy and unmotivated, but the school counselor said that the problem is a poor self-concept. A psychologist told us we needed family therapy. My neighbor is sure it's just a phase, like her youngest went through a couple of years ago."

There are fear and anxiety, too, when you think about how such a difficult child will ever make his way in the world.

"He can't get out of bed in the morning—how will he ever hold a job?"

"She's so angry and explosive; no one will ever put up with her awful temper."

"He's so down, so sad. It's like he's given up. I'm worried because I just can't imagine how he's going to face the problems of middle school—let alone high school and everything beyond that."

It is also very **painful** to listen to a depressed youngster on those rare occasions when he opens up and pours out his feelings of despair. What do you say when your child sobs, "I don't have any friends. Nobody likes me—everybody hates me"? How should you respond when he says, "I'm just no good," or "I wish I was dead; you'd be better off without me"? Later on in this chapter we will offer suggestions on how to cope with situations like these.

And then, of course, there is **guilt.** Because it is widely believed that infants are like slabs of clay that are molded and shaped by the way in which they are raised, parents of depressed children usually feel an overwhelming sense of guilt and failure. If you, yourself, suffer from depression, it's even more likely that you will quickly assume that you are to blame. "It's my fault that he's so angry and unhappy," you may have thought many times. "What did I do wrong? What should I have done differently?"

It is particularly distressing when, as is often the case, the youngster is at his very worst at home. Like many adults who suffer from mood disorders, a depressed child may be able to "keep it together" in public only to fall apart in the privacy of the family setting. Mothers, especially, are likely to be the targets of angry outbursts and verbal abuse. Many take this as proof that they are horrible parents who are somehow to blame for the child's problems. (Actually, as we explain to parents, the demands of being in a public setting, such as school, may boost certain kinds of neurochemical activity in the brain so that the child is temporarily able to function a bit better. However, when the child returns to a safe, familiar setting—and what is safer than home; who is more familiar than Mom?—his behavior deteriorates almost instantly, reflecting a sudden change in chemical activity in his brain.)

It's maddening, too, that many depressed children are at their absolute worst in the morning. If your family is like most families, mornings are hectic as family members scurry around to ready themselves for school and work. A youngster who just can't seem to get going in the morning, or who gets out of bed every day in a foul mood, throws the whole precariously balanced system out of kilter. If you, yourself, are not at your best in the morning, the chances are good that most mornings will be marred by tears, tantrums, and nasty scenes. Not at all a good way to start the day!

As if morning hassles weren't enough, parents of depressed youngsters also regularly face what some family therapists have called "the arsenic hour" at the end of the day. After a long day, the last thing you want to deal with is an irritable, demanding child who refuses to attempt his homework, complains about the food at dinner, and spends the remainder of the evening fighting with his siblings. By the time he's finally bedded down for the night—usually after a pitched battle—you are so frazzled that you feel like bursting into tears. Not at all a good way to end the day!

COPING WITH THE PROBLEMS

Before you can help your depressed child or teenager you must first have your own emotional responses under control. This is certainly a tall order because the behavior of mood-disordered youngsters seems custom-designed to push all parental buttons at once.

MANAGING YOUR OWN EMOTIONS

If you are often angry with your child—if you blow up when he defies you or seethe when he disappoints you again and again—it's certainly understandable. But, while these feelings are legitimate, you know that they contribute nothing positive to your relationship with the child nor do they help to solve the ongoing problems. On the contrary: anger clouds your ability to think. You can't come up with solutions for dealing with a troubled child if you become angry and upset yourself.

But how can you remain calm in the face of such irritating, provocative behavior? You are, after all, a human being, not a saint: how can you put your own feelings aside so that you can deal with your child's trying behavior in the most effective manner?

As a first step, it is critical to recognize that **all** children want acceptance and approval. No child chooses to suffer from a mood disorder, any more than a child with an orthopedic handicap chooses to be confined to a wheelchair. Just as we cannot blame, argue, or punish such a child into walking or running, we cannot expect the depressed child to respond to logical arguments, anger, or punishment. Some parents find this concept difficult to accept. Many would rather hold on to the belief that the child could behave differently if he tried hard enough, because this is less frightening than the awareness that the child suffers from a condition which is truly beyond his control. However, if you believe that your child is willfully misbehaving, you are likely to feel frustrated and angry and become locked into no-win power struggles. On the other hand, if you assume that your child **can't** do what is expected of him, you will look for ways to guide and assist him so that he can succeed.

When you can recognize that your child doesn't choose to feel or behave as he does, you are ready to move to the second step. This step involves putting your emotions aside, as best you can, to deal with the situation at hand. This means that you have to stop catastrophizing, since telling yourself over and over how awful things are will only make you feel worse. Instead, as child psychologist Dr. John Taylor suggests:

> Remind yourself that everyone has problems in life. There is no particular injustice in the fact that you are facing the problem. . . . Don't stop to ask fruitless questions about the justice of it all. The answer to "How could this happen to me?" is, "Very easily, because it is happening."[1]

Changing deeply entrenched patterns of thinking can be very difficult. But you can change your thinking and, in doing so, you can spare yourself a lot of unnecessary and unproductive emotional turmoil. The cognitive therapy techniques described in Chapter 5 can be very helpful in this regard, especially if you have a competent therapist as a "coach."

KEEPING YOUR MARRIAGE INTACT

Like a pebble tossed into a pond, the problems of a depressed youngster cause ripples that often extend far beyond the child himself. Sometimes the frustration and worry that parents feel are directed not toward the child but toward others. One of the most tragic forms of misdirected emotion occurs when upset parents turn on each other, each blaming the other for the problem. One parent (typically the father) might complain, "You're too lenient with him; you let him get away with murder," while the other (usually the mother) counters with, "You're too hard on him. You're always yelling at him and threatening him."

We know that most children tend to behave somewhat better for their fathers than for their mothers. (Who doesn't remember Mom's ultimate weapon: "Just you wait until your father comes home"?) With depressed youngsters, as we noted, mothers are likely to be the target of the worst of the child's behavior. How demoralizing for the exhausted mother who has just spent hours coping with an angry, irritable child to hear her husband say, "How come you have so many problems with him? He never pulls that stuff with me. Why can't you make him behave?"

In other ways, too, the presence of a depressed youngster in the family can place a strain on a marriage. The cost of treatment is high, often stressing the family budget. There is also the cost in terms of time. Who will drive the child to his therapy appointments? Who will follow through to see that he takes his medication on time? Who will attend meetings at the school? On a day-to-day basis, who will field calls from the school when problems come up?

Marital problems are particularly likely to exist when, as is often the case in families with a depressed child, one or even both parents suffer from a mood disorder themselves. The irritability and withdrawal which accompany depression create severe problems in close interpersonal relationships, often resulting in an escalating pattern of negative exchanges which we have dubbed a "dance of dysfunction." Unfortunately, we know that depressed people tend to marry people who also have psychiatric problems.[2] When this happens—when a depressed person has a psychiatrically disturbed spouse—the depressed person's own symptoms worsen and family disruption is even more likely.

TAKING CARE OF YOURSELF

Clearly, parenting a depressed youngster can be a herculean task, so it would be astonishing if you didn't occasionally feel exhausted and dispirited. However, if you often feel irritable

and out of sorts, if you are always exhausted and overwhelmed, if nothing seems fun or worthwhile anymore, you,
too, may be suffering from depression.

As we pointed out earlier, your own depression will inevitably affect your ability to interact with your depressed youngster. Since depression saps your energy and your enthusiasm,
your interaction with your child is likely to be constricted.
You won't respond as quickly and warmly to your child's appropriate and adaptive behavior, but you are likely to respond
more punitively to even minor transgressions. These changes
in your behavior contribute in subtle but very powerful ways
to your child's problems, virtually ensuring that the "dance of
dysfunction" will continue.

Therefore, we think that, if you are the depressed parent
of a depressed child, the single most important thing you can
do for your child is to obtain effective treatment for yourself.
Only when you are feeling your best can you begin to help
your child with his or her problems.

THE REST OF THE FAMILY

HELPING SIBLINGS COPE. Did you ever wonder who came up
with the silly notion that brothers and sisters should just naturally get along in peace and harmony? Whoever he was, he
was surely an only child!

As anyone with rudimentary knowledge of animal behavior can tell you, siblings of all species are pitted from the start
in an intense and never ending contest to be Number One in
their parents' favor. No matter how much love, attention, and
material resources are available, children will still compete relentlessly for the position of Numero Uno. That's just the way
Mother Nature designed us.

Natural and normal though sibling competition might be,
it is nevertheless a serious problem for parents, who find it
distressing when the competition results in their children in-
flicting emotional and physical pain on each other. It is baf-

fling, too: you know that you have enough love to go around and you know that you treat all of your children equitably. Why can't they see that and cease the endless battling and tattling? Why the constant cries of "No fair" and "You like him better"?

To help you understand sibling rivalry from a child's perspective, Adele Faber and Elaine Mazlish, authors of the wonderful book *Siblings Without Rivalry*,[3] offer this very pointed analogy. Imagine, they suggest, that your spouse suddenly announces that, because you are such a wonderful spouse, he/she has decided to have another spouse "just like you." When the new spouse arrives, friends and family exclaim ecstatically over the newcomer: "How cute!" and "How adorable!" Your time with your spouse is now limited, because the newcomer, too, demands time and attention. When the newcomer needs clothing, your spouse raids your closet for your outgrown clothes, and then, upset that you are unwilling to share, accuses you of being selfish.

Now, what would your reaction be under these circumstances? It's probably no exaggeration to say that you would feel like punching the newcomer's lights!

And punch each other is exactly what siblings do. They also kick, bite, pinch, hit with blunt objects, and so on. The rates of sibling violence in households across the country are high—so high, in fact, that researchers categorize such violence as pandemic; that is, it occurs in a majority of children as they grow up.[4] Research shows, too, that rates are even higher in families of depressed children: depressed youngsters have more antagonistic relationships and more frequent fights with their siblings than nondepressed children.[5]

It is our experience as clinicians that intense and extreme antagonism toward siblings is a red flag which often signals the presence of depression in a youngster. Sometimes parents even trace the onset of the older child's emotional and behavioral problems to the birth of a sibling. Certainly the arrival of a new baby is accompanied by changes in interaction between the mother and the older child. Children with difficult temperaments often do not react well to change. They may become more difficult, miserable, and withdrawn, while their mothers become more punitive and less playful and attentive.[6] It is no wonder, then, that older children may develop intense and long-lasting feelings of resentment and antagonism toward the intruder.

Since you certainly don't plan to "return" the younger child (who may now be a teenager), what can you do about it? First, as Louis Bates Ames, cofounder of the Gesell Institute, advises, don't play the fairness game.[7] Don't get into lengthy debates about whether or not something is "fair" and don't go into long-winded explanations of how hard you try to be evenhanded. Instead, recognize the complaint for what it is: the child's need for some special attention and support.

You can best meet the child's need in a direct fashion. Listen sympathetically to the child's complaints. You don't have to agree and you don't have to come up with solutions (most of which wouldn't work anyway). Often, the simple act of listening closely, without judgment or interruption, is enough to calm your child and reassure him that his feelings are important to you. For a host of excellent ideas and clear directions for putting them into practice, we refer you to *Siblings Without Rivalry*.

Finally, there is the question of just how much cooperation and understanding you can reasonably expect the other children in the family to extend to the depressed child. While this depends to some extent on the age, sex, and personality of each of the children—in general, there is usually more rivalry between siblings who are closest in age, for example—parents are likely to hope for more compassion from brothers and sisters than the youngsters are able to deliver. Children are "bottom line" oriented: the explanation "He can't help it" doesn't mean much. The bottom line is "He did it—period."

Instead of appealing to reason or to the child's sense of moral responsibility, you would probably do better to employ some of the behavior management methods described below (see p. 154) to improve the way in which your other children behave toward your depressed child, and vice versa. If the payoff for cooperation outweighs the entertainment value of fighting with each other, children are much more likely to cooperate. The old behavior modification dictum "Catch them being good" is particularly apt: instead of waiting until your children demand your attention with fighting and screaming, make it a point to lavish attention on them when they are playing cooperatively together. Praise will help; so will special treats. Often, however, the most potent reinforcer is joining the children in their ongoing activity: remember that competition for your attention is what the battle is really all about to begin with.

THE EXTENDED FAMILY. Wouldn't it be wonderful if, in the midst of all of these trials, you could pick up the phone and get sympathy and support from your mother or your father or your sister? It would indeed, but the reality is that many parents of depressed youngsters cannot turn to members of their extended families for support in trying times. In fact, when they try, they may be rebuffed, encountering criticism and blame instead of support, because family members may be so caught up in their own problems that they can give little in the way of help or understanding.

> "My brother and his wife stopped by the other day to drop off some things from my mom. It had been an awful morning: from the time Seth got out of bed until the time he left for school, it was nothing but whine, fuss, and scream. My brother arrived just as I was pushing Seth out the door to catch the school bus. My brother watched the whole scene from the driveway and then, after Seth was gone, he delivered a ten-minute lecture on how I spoil Seth and how he would handle things very differently if Seth were his kid. His little tirade reminded me of when I was a kid and how my parents would go on and on about how I had messed up on something. After he left, I just sat on the kitchen floor and cried."

Even when family members are supportive and understanding, you might still hesitate to participate in family get-togethers. No one will directly criticize you, but you cringe when you think about the silent comparisons that will be made between your child and those of other family members. Because you avoid family gatherings, you miss out on potentially enjoyable events which could serve to recharge your own low batteries.

MANAGING PROBLEM BEHAVIOR

In Chapter 5 we briefly outlined the principles of behavior modification, an approach which uses positive and negative consequences in a systematic fashion to produce changes in behavior. We noted that, while behavioral techniques alone cannot serve as a comprehensive treatment program for depressed youngsters, parents can use these principles to improve behavior in the home. Since many excellent books for parents provide detailed explanations and examples of behavior modification methods, we will give only an overview here, highlighting the most important features.

USING CONSEQUENCES TO CHANGE BEHAVIOR

Recall from our earlier discussion that behavior is strengthened by positive consequences (reinforcers) which follow immediately on the heels of the behavior. If, for example, your wave to a neighbor is met with a friendly smile and a cheery "Hello," you will be even more likely to extend a greeting to your neighbor the next time you see him.

On the other hand, you wouldn't be much inclined to wave and smile at a neighbor who never returned your greetings. And you certainly would cease your efforts instantly if, in return, your neighbor swore at you or threw rocks over the fence! From this example, you can see that, if a particular behavior never produces positive consequences, or if it consistently results in negative or unpleasant consequences, the behavior will be weakened and ultimately eliminated.

As parents, when we think about managing problem behavior, we usually think first of putting a stop to the behavior by providing negative consequences (punishment). This is unfortunate because a vast scientific literature attests to the fact that positive consequences are really the most powerful tools in bringing about long-lasting changes in behavior, while punishment is usually an ineffective way to change behavior.

Think about it: how many times have you punished your children for leaving their rooms in disarray or their bikes in the driveway? How many times have you punished them for name-calling, teasing, or hitting each other? How well has it worked? Are all bedrooms now spotless? Are bikes always stored safely in the shed? Is everything now sweetness and light among your children? (We didn't think so!)

The problem with punishment is that it conveys a limited amount of information: it tells the child what **not** to do—at least while you're looking—but it doesn't suggest or promote more acceptable kinds of behavior. Punishment can backfire, too, actually leading to increases in undesirable behavior such as tantrums and aggressive behavior. It is also likely to result in ugly power struggles between parent and child, especially if the child is a teenager who will do almost anything to avoid losing face. With a depressed teenager, it is particularly important to avoid such escalations: as we discussed in Chapter 7, angry altercations between depressed youngsters and their parents or other authority figures have been identified as a precipitant of suicide in vulnerable young people.

POSITIVE CONSEQUENCES. A program which emphasizes positive consequences is not only more effective than one which stresses negative consequences: such an approach has special relevance to the depressed child, since research indicates that depressed youngsters are on a "thin diet" of positive reinforcement. Studies have shown, for example, that parents of depressed youngsters are generous with criticism but quite stingy with praise and other forms of positive reinforcement, doling it out infrequently and then only when the child meets a very high standard of behavior.[8]

Studies have also shown that families of depressed children engage in relatively few pleasant social or recreational activities, so these children have fewer opportunities to receive reinforcement from such activities.[9] Since research also shows a direct link between a child's mood and the time he spends engaged in pleasant activities,[10] it isn't surprising at all that the mood of these youngsters is so low.

Parents sometimes worry that a behavior management program built around positive consequences will bankrupt them, since their thoughts turn quickly to trips to shopping centers and amusement parks. But reinforcers don't have to be elaborate or expensive in order to be effective. They must, however, be carefully selected to appeal to the individual child. With depressed children, this can be tricky because one of the classic symptoms of depression is a loss of pleasure in previously enjoyable activities. To help you and your youngster identify potentially reinforcing consequences, consult the "Fun Things to Do" schedule in Appendix C.

Once you've identified some promising reinforcers, you can begin to target behaviors you'd like to change. The simplest way to do this is to make a list of your youngster's undesirable behaviors, since these are the behaviors that come to mind most readily. Then, turn each of these behaviors into its opposite. For example, "Isolates herself in her room" becomes "Spends time with family"; "Won't get out of bed" becomes "Dressed and ready for breakfast at eight o'clock"; and "Fights with brother" becomes "Plays cooperatively with brother."

Armed with a list of target behaviors and a list of reinforcers, you are ready to embark on a behavior change program. We suggest that you begin modestly, limiting the scope of your program to one or two behaviors initially. Professionals who use behavior modification methods with children sometimes suggest that parents use point programs in which a number of problem behaviors are targeted simultaneously. We have found, however, that these programs are often too complicated and time-consuming for many parents, especially single-parent families and families in which both parents work outside the home.

Here are some other points to remember when you begin a behavior change program with your youngster.

- **Timing is critical.** The most powerful consequences are those which follow the behavior immediately; consequences which come later in time are much less powerful in changing behavior. For example, instead of promising the child a new video game if he can go for a month without hitting his siblings, buy the video game and let the child rent it on a daily or weekly basis, as determined by his behavior that day or that week.

- **Be generous:** reinforce often and for small improvements. We noted that parents of depressed children often expect a very high level of performance before they dispense praise or rewards. Don't do this! Instead, think of the target behavior as the top step of a stairway which your child must climb, step by step. If he doesn't receive any reinforcement when he climbs steps one, two, and three, he may give up before he reaches the fourth step. For the depressed child, in particular, this will be just one more failure—one more indication to him that he can't succeed at anything he tries.

  Rather than demanding that a child go all week without fighting with his siblings, set the initial goal as a morning—or even an hour—of peaceful coexistence. Once this goal has been met over the course of a couple of days, you can gradually extend the period of time, little by little.

- **Use lots of praise.** It's funny: although we all agree with the aphorism "Talk is cheap," you wouldn't guess this

from the paltry amount of praise and positive feedback
most of us dispense to those around us. Smiles, winks,
and exclamations of "Nice job!" don't cost a penny but
they can yield terrific dividends. These positive consequences are easy to use and they can be delivered on the
spot to reinforce desirable behavior. They even have the
added bonus of making you feel a bit better every time
you deliver one!

If, like most of us, you are in the habit of doling
out a lot more criticism than praise, you might want to
try this little exercise. Take an index card and divide it
into two columns marked "Praise" and "Criticism."
Carry the card with you at all times and make a check
in the appropriate column each time you praise or criticize your child for his behavior. After three or four
days, tally the checks in each column. It's likely that the
checks in the "Criticism" column far outnumber the
checks in the "Praise" column. If that is the case, you
can engineer consequences to change your own behavior. You might decide, for example, to deny yourself a
second cup of coffee or a look at the paper until you
have dispensed a certain number of positive comments
to your child.

NEGATIVE CONSEQUENCES. As we discussed, there are
many problems associated with using punishment to control
the behavior of all children—and the depressed child, in particular. However, this doesn't mean that you should completely abandon the use of negative consequences and rely
solely on positive consequences to manage your child's behavior. That's not only unrealistic, since real life is not all positive
consequences; it wouldn't work, even if you could manage to
do it.

We do think, however, that you should make changes in
the way you think about and use negative consequences. For
openers, we suggest that you eliminate the word "punish-

ment" from your vocabulary—even from your thinking. The point here is that you are not a police officer or a prison warden: you are a parent whose role is to teach and to guide. Harsh or painful consequences won't help your child see the light: they will just hurt and humiliate him. Since depressed youngsters are particularly sensitive to criticism and negative consequences,[11] you certainly want to take this into account and deliver negative feedback in a low-key manner.

The method known as "Time Out" is an excellent example of a negative consequence that doesn't involve anger, pain, or humiliation. This easy-to-use method, which has gained well-deserved popularity with parents and teachers, involves isolating the child in a boring place for a few minutes immediately after he misbehaves. Any boring place in the house will do nicely—a chair in the dining room, the child's bedroom, the back stairs. We used to tell parents to be sure that the Time Out area contained no diversions, since it was thought that this would defeat the purpose of Time Out. However, more recent research suggests that this might not be as important as we once thought: current thinking is that simply interrupting the child's ongoing activity is usually sufficient to drive home the point.

Don't think of Time Out as punishment and don't present it that way to your child. Instead, explain that Time Out is "quiet time," a few minutes in which your child can think about his unacceptable behavior and come up with some good ideas for how he might handle things better the next time.

The Time Out procedure is a very effective way to counter obnoxious behavior, since it provides both you and your child with an opportunity to cool off. This is particularly important with depressed youngsters, since some seem almost driven to provoke fights and arguments. (We speculate that such youngsters are actually engaging in a kind of self-medication, in which loud, angry battles trigger the release of certain neurochemicals which temporarily relieve symptoms of depression.)

One problem with Time Out is that it is an all-or-nothing approach; that is, the child is either sent to Time Out or he isn't. This poses a dilemma when, knowing your child as well as you do, you see trouble brewing but the child hasn't actually done anything that would merit Time Out—yet. If you sent him to Time Out for every little infraction, such as "accidentally" bumping into his sister, he would never see the world outside of his bedroom. On the other hand, if you don't intervene early in the cycle, you know that it's only a matter of time before you have one more crisis on your hands.

Dr. Tom Phelan, a clinical psychologist who specializes in working with children and adolescents, has come up with a modification of Time Out which he calls "1-2-3: Magic!" Using Dr. Phelan's procedure, you don't nag and you don't threaten but you do give a warning: holding up one finger, you say, "That's one." If the behavior doesn't stop within a few seconds, you proceed to "That's two." If the child persists, you say, "That's three," and the child is sent to Time Out. For more detailed information, as well as a wealth of practical suggestions for dealing with children's behavior problems, we highly recommend Dr. Phelan's book, *1-2-3: Magic! Training Your Preschoolers and Preteens to Do What You Want.*[12]

IMPROVING COMMUNICATION IN THE FAMILY

In preceding chapters we described disturbed patterns of interaction and communication in the families of depressed children and adolescents. We also noted that a goal of family therapy is to improve communication by teaching family members to modify their communication style—teaching them, for example, how to express feelings in a nondestructive way, how to express understanding of the other person's point of view, and how to negotiate disputes. As parents, you can do much to keep the lines of communication open by following the suggestions below.

- **Be brief.** Children tend to have short attention spans, especially when communiqués from parents are concerned. Keep your directions short and simple.

- **Be direct.** Don't give vague or confusing directions or directions which invite an argument. Instead of "Don't run" (to which the child is likely to respond "I wasn't running; I was skipping") tell the child exactly what you want him to do (i.e., "Walk!")

- **Make "I" statements.** Statements that begin with the word "you" can instantly put a youngster on the defensive because such statements are often threatening or accusatory.

  "You are so rude."

  "You make me so mad."

  "I" statements which simply describe your thoughts and feelings have much greater impact.

  "When you yell at me in public I feel embarrassed and angry."

  "I get upset when you hit your sister. It hurts me to see someone I love hurting someone else I love."

- **Be an active listener.** Listening involves more than simply taking in a message. Effective listening includes letting the other person know that his message has been received and understood. A good listener communicates attention and interest through eye contact, facial expressions, and verbal "following" (e.g., "Um-hm," "I see").

Active listening also involves letting the other person know that you understand and accept the feelings he has about the situation. This is particularly important when your youngster is angry or upset. Think back to the last time you were angry or worried or frightened. Did it help to have someone:

- offer off-the-cuff advice? ("Just ignore him when he does that.")

- argue with you? ("I'm sure he didn't really mean it.")

- tell you to calm down and not make such a big deal of the situation? ("Oh, come on; it's silly to be that angry about such a little thing.")

In each case, the response was meant to be helpful. But was it? Probably not, because responses like these amount to little more than "put-downs." Jumping in with advice—which parents are particularly likely to do—is like saying, "You aren't smart enough to know how to handle the situation so I will tell you what to do." This approach not only doesn't work, since pat solutions seldom solve much; it also does nothing to encourage your child to think of his own solutions to the problem. And telling a child, "It's not that bad," tells the child that his problem doesn't exist or that he is silly to be concerned about it.

When children are emotionally aroused, what they really want most from their parents is some understanding and validation of their feelings—something along the lines of "I can see how that would make you furious," or "Wow, that must have really been scary!" or "Oh, no. You must have felt awful!" This doesn't mean that parents must take the child's side in the problem or that they agree with the child's view of the situation: the nuts and bolts of resolving the problem may still need to be addressed. Often, however, just having Mom or Dad hear him out in a sympathetic and nonjudgmental way goes a long way toward solving a youngster's problem.

Although active listening appears easy, considerable practice is required to use it comfortably and with skill. Two good books on active listening for parents are Hiam Ginott's *Between Parent and Child**; and Adele Faber and Elaine Mazlish's *How to Talk So Kids Will Listen and Listen So Kids Will Talk.*†

---

* New York: Macmillan, 1975.
† New York: Avon, 1982.

HELPING THE CHILD SUCCEED SOCIALLY

If your youngster has had a hard time making and keeping friends, as is the case with so many depressed children and adolescents, you've certainly shared the pain of his social rejection and you have probably tried to help in all sorts of ways. If he is an isolated child who spends long hours in front of the television or the computer, you've probably talked yourself hoarse exhorting him to call some friends and arrange to get together with them. If he is a socially rejected child who is teased and actively avoided by other children, you've probably tried to help him learn to cope with teasing ("Just ignore them when they tease you" is the advice adults usually dispense). You've almost certainly tried to get your child involved in such social activities as scouting, athletic teams, and various clubs, hoping that something will click—that he will be accepted by the other youngsters and find his social niche.

If all of your attempts have been unsuccessful, it's time to step back and take careful stock of the situation. What is it that keeps your child from having successful and enjoyable peer relationships? Is your child so irritable and explosive that he drives away potential friends with his angry outbursts? Is his self-esteem so low that he interprets anything his peers do as indicating a rejection of him? Is he so shy and withdrawn that the very prospect of playing with other children causes him acute distress?

These problems can and should be addressed in your child's therapy. It is likely, for example, that cognitive therapy can be helpful in changing the way in which the child interprets the motives and behavior of others. Treatment with medication can often reduce irritability and explosiveness so that the child is no longer apt to alienate others with his unpleasant and unpredictable behavior.

For children who are socially inept or who have problems with peer relations, social-skills training would certainly seem to offer a useful intervention. In fact, as we discussed in Chapter 5, social-skills training is usually included as an adjunctive procedure in the treatment of depressed children and adolescents.

How effective is social-skills training? On the face of it, this approach to remediating the social problems of depressed youngsters would certainly seem to have much to offer. Judging by the current popularity of this approach, parents apparently think so too. We agree that social-skills training can confer benefits but we believe that certain caveats are in order. Parents should be aware that brief, clinic-based training programs which don't include specific follow-through in the child's natural environment are seldom successful. On the other hand, when parents are actively involved as cotherapists who can monitor the child's social progress in the real world, social-skills training can be expected to yield much more in the way of benefits.

What else can you do to help? Again, any interventions will depend on the specific problems you have identified as standing in the way of your child's ability to get along well with his peers. Some suggestions follow.

- Help your child improve his play skills. If your child doesn't know the rules of the games his peers like to play, teach him the rules and practice playing the games with him. If he lacks the necessary skills—if he can't throw or catch a ball or swim or ride a bike—arrange to have him learn these all-important skills. Since most parents are not good tutors for their own children, you might want to let someone else take over. Sports camps which emphasize teaching fundamentals in a noncompetitive environment are ideal. If camps like these are not available in your area, call the coach at the local high school and ask if he can recommend a high school athlete who would be interested in earning extra money by coaching your child.

- Plan activities that are attractive to other children. Before other children can learn to like your child, they must first have an opportunity to get to know him. In our experience, the old adage "Familiarity breeds contempt" should be consigned to the dump. Instead, as social psychologists tell us, we find that familiarity is much more likely to foster understanding, tolerance, and acceptance—even liking! You can take advantage of this by planning exciting activities and inviting a neighbor child or one of your child's classmates to come along and share the fun. Trips to the theater, amusement parks, and sports events are fun for children. So are swimming parties, movies, and dinners at your child's favorite fast food restaurants.

  If you decide to host parties and sleepovers, be sure that you provide the very latest in video games, movies, and lots of food that children and teenagers enjoy. This isn't "buying" friends for your youngster; it's investing in his success. By making your child's company valuable to other children, you are creating opportunities for him to make friends and learn to get along with others.

- Avoid a sink-or-swim approach. If you want your child to experience success in a group, don't just throw him into the situation and hope for the best. Instead, provide carefully monitored opportunities for the child to experience pleasurable and successful contacts with peers. In any group, be sure that you know the adult leaders and be sure they understand your child's special needs. Better yet, get involved as a leader so you can be on the scene to provide help and support as needed.

Teachers who have socially isolated youngsters in their classrooms can certainly help too. In many ways, this is an easier task for teachers than for parents, since teachers have ready-made opportunities to help the child interact with his peers. Suggestions for teachers are outlined in Chapter 9.

NINE

What Can the Teacher Do?

The Depressed Child in School

DO YOU REMEMBER—really remember—what it was like to be a child? To have to face, day in and day out, the demands of a world in which you had little or no say? In no other area of a child's life are these demands so relentless and so unremitting as they are in school; in no other setting is a child quite so vulnerable to having his weaknesses and deficits exposed to the eyes of others. Developmental pediatrician Mel Levine, a man who is exquisitely sensitive to children's feelings, puts it this way:

> From the moment school-age children emerge from the bed covers each day until their safe return to that security, they are preoccupied with the avoidance of humiliation at all cost. They have a constant need to look good, to sidestep embarrassment, and to gain respect, especially from their peers.[1]

Children, he says, must struggle constantly to meet the expectations of so many people. On a daily basis they must juggle what's expected of them from their parents, their teachers, and their age-mates. Often, these expectations are in conflict, not only with each other, but with the child's actual abilities in terms of meeting them.

Unlike adults, children cannot arrange their lives to avoid situations in which their weaknesses are exposed. In fact, among all of the platitudes that adults mouth to children, surely one of the silliest is the comparison between the adult's role as a worker and the child's role as a student (i.e., "Mom and Dad go to work each day at our jobs: your job is to go to school and do the best you can"). As adults, we can choose to pursue employment in fields in which we lead with our strengths. But children don't have this option: every child, regardless of his innate strengths and weaknesses, is expected to perform daily in an impossibly broad arena. He is judged by his teachers (and by his peers) on his abilities in areas which range from arithmetic to art, from music to mapmaking, and from reading to running track.

No child can excel in all areas but, while the child who can't sing will be embarrassed only occasionally in music class, the child who has learning disabilities or attentional difficulties will be frustrated and embarrassed for the better part of every day he is in school.

Youngsters who have social problems also find school a particularly painful experience. Each day brings anxiety about whether anyone will sit with them on the bus, play with them at recess, or talk to them at lunch. In the case of youngsters who are actively rejected by other children, there is the very real fear that they will be taunted, teased, humiliated—even physically assaulted—by their peers.

For depressed children, many of whom suffer from one or more of these problems, social and academic failures are only further proof that they can do nothing right and that they can never hope to succeed. In fact, in many cases, youngsters with

such difficulties actually seem to become depressed as a result
of their social and academic struggles in school.

THE TEACHER'S ROLE

IDENTIFYING THE DEPRESSED CHILD

Since children spend the better part of their waking hours in
the classroom, one might think that teachers are in an ideal
position to spot the warning signals of depression in their students. Unfortunately, although teachers are very competent at
identifying children who suffer from the disruptive disorders,
such as Attention-Deficit Disorder, they are much less skilled
at recognizing those who suffer from depression and anxiety.
Teachers are not in a position to observe such symptoms of
depression as sleep problems and loss of appetite and, as we
noted earlier, most depressed children do not call attention to
themselves by acting up in class. Nor are they likely to share
their fears, worries, sadness, or suicidal thoughts with a
teacher, no matter how close the teacher-child relationship.

What, then, are the signs that should alert a teacher to the
possibility that a youngster suffers from depression?

RED FLAGS

- Somatic complaints: If a youngster often complains of
  headaches, stomachaches, or other physical aches and
  pains, teachers should be alert to the possibility of a
  depressive illness. Frequent requests to go to the nurse's
  office for various ailments are clear signals that something is wrong.

- Poor frustration tolerance: Children and adolescents
  who suffer from depression have little in the way of
  ability to "bounce back" from disappointment. Many
  are perfectionists who fall apart in tears or angry outbursts when little things go wrong—when they make a

mistake, for example, or when they are otherwise thwarted in pursuit of a goal.

• Lethargy, listlessness: Youngsters who frequently fall asleep in class or appear to have no energy or enthusiasm for activities which other children find enjoyable may be suffering from depression. In adolescents, these symptoms may signal drug or alcohol abuse. In either case, there is cause for concern and a need to alert parents to the problem.

• Social isolation, peer problems: Depressed children, as we have noted in earlier sections, are particularly likely to have difficulty with friendships and peer acceptance. This is certainly not always the case—some depressed youngsters are well liked and accepted by their peers. We believe, however, that teachers should **never** ignore the plight of youngsters who have peer problems, especially since there is much the teacher can do to help (see p. 170).

• Conditions which often coexist with depression, such as Attention-Deficit Disorder or learning disabilities: as we have discussed, a child who has one or more of the conditions which commonly coexist with depression is apt to be a "sitting duck" for the development of a mood disorder.

• Midyear slump: If a youngster's performance drops off dramatically during the winter months, don't be too quick to write it off to postholiday letdown. If this is a recurrent pattern, it suggests the possibility that a seasonal mood disorder (Seasonal Affective Disorder) might underlie the seasonal variations in the child's performance.

THE TEACHER-CHILD RELATIONSHIP

Next to his relationship with his parents, a youngster's relationships with his teachers are among the most significant associations he has with adults during the childhood and teenage years. Indeed, when adults who suffered from childhood learning, emotional, or attentional problems are asked what helped them succeed in spite of their difficulties, more than a few recall a teacher whose concern and caring helped them begin to believe in themselves.

Of course, not every teacher is right for every student: it's patently ridiculous to think otherwise. Some teachers take special delight in working with active, rambunctious youngsters; these teachers are quite gifted in helping such youngsters direct and focus their high levels of energy. Other teachers, by virtue of their personal style, are particularly sensitive and responsive to the needs of the quiet, withdrawn youngster who might otherwise be overlooked and fall through the proverbial cracks. Some teachers enjoy exchanging repartee with bright, verbal youngsters; others consider these children "smart alecs" and find their behavior offensive. In an ideal world, the possibility of a mismatch between child and teacher would be recognized and procedures to correct such a mismatch would be readily available, with no blame attached to either teacher or child. In the real world, however, when mismatches occur, teacher and child are condemned to a miserable school year together.

When, in our clinical practice, we encounter such mismatches, we do not hesitate to recommend that the child be switched to a different teacher—sometimes even to a different school. It's true that school administrators often resist such a recommendation, fearing that it reflects poorly on the teacher. We have found, however, that if parents present the situation as a mismatch rather than simply blaming or berating the teacher, administrators are less reluctant to move the child to another setting in which there is a greater likelihood of success.

HELPING THE DEPRESSED CHILD
WITH PEER PROBLEMS

Whether or not a youngster is accepted by his classmates can be a make-or-break factor in the child's attitude toward school. Unfortunately, as we have seen, many depressed youngsters are woefully deficient in social skills and, as a result, they are actively rejected or just simply ignored by other children.

What can the classroom teacher do to help a depressed youngster gain social acceptance among his classmates? Much more than you might think! For the most part, teachers themselves don't seem to realize how much influence they have over the nonacademic aspects of daily life in school. This influence can be exercised quite explicitly: teachers can, for example, take time to discuss and describe the social behavior which they expect from their students, in the classroom as well as elsewhere in the school. They can make it quite clear that cooperation and mutual support are acceptable and praiseworthy behaviors, while aggressive behavior, teasing, and putdowns will be met with stern disapproval.

Indirectly, teachers can instruct their students in treating others with compassion, kindness, and respect by modeling these attitudes in their own behavior. The teacher who praises publicly and who corrects gently and in private shows by example how children should treat each other (see p. 175).

Teachers can help, too, by praising other children for including the depressed child in their work or play activities. At the early elementary school level, direct praise is helpful: a teacher might say, for example, "Chad, I really like to see you playing with [names of other children]." To the child's playmates, the teacher could also say, "It looks like you're having a lot of fun playing with Chad. Is there anything you need to

help you work on this project?" This special attention from
the teacher can go a long way toward helping the isolated or
rejected child gain greater acceptance among his classmates.

With older children, more subtle expressions of approval
are necessary. When the depressed child is working or playing
with others, the teacher can help by making positive comments about the activity and the participants. If, for example,
Ashley is working with her classmates on a project about sea
creatures, the teacher could comment on how hard everyone is
working, singling Ashley out for particular praise for her efforts.

Based on his research, psychologist James Barclay offers
these additional suggestions for classroom teachers.[2]

- Plan classroom activities in which the depressed child
  can participate with other children as an equal or even
  a superior. For example, the class could put on mini-
  plays: the depressed child would be cast in the role of
  the hero and subsequently commended by the teacher
  for a brilliant performance. Educators tell us that mini-
  plays are an enjoyable teaching device which can be
  incorporated easily into the teaching of virtually any
  subject to help the subject "come alive" for the students.

- Make use of activities which involve mutual cooperation, rather than competition. Dr. Barclay offers the
  example of a spelling game in which members of each
  team have a letter printed on a piece of paper; when a
  word is called out, team members must arrange themselves so that the word is spelled correctly.

  Dr. David Guevremont, a psychologist at the University of Massachusetts Medical Center, believes that
  cooperative learning tasks are great for promoting positive peer interactions with all sorts of children.[3] Cooperative learning tasks are those which involve a small
  group of children working together toward a common

goal (e.g., building a model, solving a practical problem) so that each child must make a contribution toward achieving the goal. Dr. Guevremont correctly observes that children who participate in cooperative learning tasks show greater liking for one another and an increase in positive feelings toward one another.

• Avoid the common mistake of conferring choice classroom jobs, such as hall monitor or errand runner, on the more successful students. These children, who usually tend to be among the more popular children as well as the most academically accomplished, need little to bolster their self-esteem or to keep them motivated to perform at high levels. Instead, since these coveted classroom jobs bestow a certain amount of prestige, they should be used as resources both to reward the depressed youngster for small steps toward improvement and to confer higher social status on the child.

• Intervene actively to break up cliques. As adults, we decry the tendency of children to form little packs, or "popular groups," whose most important and pressing activity seems to be excluding others from the inner circle. Although teachers often feel helpless to take action against this common problem, Dr. Barclay believes that teachers can do much to intervene. He suggests that teachers break up existing cliques by avoiding the practice of allowing children to form their own work groups and activity groups. When this happens, he points out, the popular children stick together and the less popular children are left out. Instead, the teacher should organize groups in such a way that the unpopular child is paired with one or two of the most popular children in the class, because popularity tends to "rub off."

MANAGING PROBLEM BEHAVIOR IN THE CLASSROOM

As we noted earlier, most depressed children do not engage in disruptive or defiant behavior in the classroom. A minority do, however, and a teacher must be prepared to work effectively with these children as well as with those whose depression manifests itself in more subtle ways, such as poor attention in the classroom and problems completing work.

The importance of immediate feedback—especially positive feedback—in managing the behavior of the depressed child was discussed in Chapter 8. Remember that, if feedback is to be most effective in promoting behavior change, it must be dispensed frequently and it must follow each small step toward improvement.

Positive feedback is much more powerful and efficient than negative feedback in bringing about long-term changes in behavior. Unfortunately, teachers tend to be as shortsighted as the rest of us: in spite of countless studies documenting the effectiveness of positive reinforcement, research shows that teachers still give much more criticism and correction than praise and positive feedback. In fact, after about the first or second grade, the amount of teacher approval meted out for appropriate classroom behavior is virtually **nonexistent.**

If you're a teacher, we ask you to stop and think: when was the last time you gave a little wink to a child who was obviously paying attention to your lecture or your directions? When was the last time you said:

- "I love the way you're working so hard on your journal" instead of "Stop playing with your pencil and get to work"?

- "Finished already? This looks like you put in some real effort" instead of "Please stop staring out the window and finish your math paper"?

We don't mean to imply that negative feedback can or should be entirely eliminated: for most children, the best results are obtained with a combination of frequent positive consequences for appropriate behavior and mild negative consequences for inappropriate behavior. We do, however, believe that the use of negative feedback should be minimized; that, when it is necessary to administer it, it should be delivered as quietly and unobtrusively as possible; and that it should certainly take a back seat to an emphasis on positive feedback.

To help teachers remember to increase positives, we suggest the method described for parents in Chapter 8. Using an index card with columns marked "Praise" and "Criticism," a tally of each kind of feedback can be kept on a daily basis. The goal, of course, is to increase the former and decrease the latter.

The benefit to the teacher who uses a more positive approach is that, as the teacher's behavior changes, so does that of the child. There are fringe benefits too: researchers tell us that, even if a teacher targets only one or two children in the class and concentrates on changing the ratio of positives to negatives with them, other children in the class also show improvements in behavior. Finally, by targeting the depressed youngster in such a fashion, the teacher increases the child's status in the eyes of his peers—certainly an important side effect with depressed children, since so many have such low social status.

We noted that depressed youngsters are more apt to have "passive" classroom problems, such as poor attention and concentration, with subsequent failure to complete their class work. Teachers can help with these problems, too. An excellent way to do this is to use an "attention span tape," an audio cassette tape which plays a tone at variable intervals.* While

* A good "attention span tape," called the Listen, Look, and Think Program, is available from the A.D.D. WareHouse in Plantation, FL. Their toll-free number is 1-800-233-9273.

working on his class work (or on his homework), the child listens for the tone and, when the tone sounds, he makes a check on a paper tally to indicate whether or not he was paying attention to his work. Such a tape, which research has shown to be effective in helping inattentive youngsters stay on-task, can be used with individual children or—better yet— with an entire class.

ACADEMIC ACCOMMODATIONS AND
SPECIAL PLACEMENT

In the past, a youngster who was underachieving or actually failing in school in spite of apparent good intelligence was written off as "lazy," "immature," or "unmotivated." These youngsters often were forced to repeat a grade but, since there was no clear understanding of why the youngster had failed the first time around, this solution was seldom helpful. Many of these young people simply dropped out of school and drifted into low-paying jobs, eking out a marginal existence on the fringes of society.

In 1975, the passage of Public Law 94-142, known as the Education of the Handicapped Act, changed all of this. This law, since reauthorized in 1990 as the Individuals with Disabilities Education Act (IDEA), removed the onus for failure to learn from the child's shoulders and placed responsibility on the public school system to provide special services for all children who need them in order to succeed in school.

INDIVIDUALS WITH DISABILITIES ACT: IDEA

This law guarantees a free and appropriate education for children between the ages of three and twenty-one who suffer from thirteen specific disabling conditions. These conditions include deafness, visual impairments, speech/language delays, serious emotional disturbance, orthopedic problems, learning disabilities, and other health-related conditions. (Although depression is not specifically listed as a disabling condition, many depressed children are still covered under IDEA—see pages 178–79 for details.)

The law provides a very detailed set of eligibility standards for each of these handicapping conditions. It also describes procedures for identifying and evaluating youngsters suspected of having a handicapping condition, including a comprehensive educational and psychological evaluation conducted by a multidisciplinary team. If it is determined that a youngster has a handicapping condition, the school is obligated to provide all necessary special education services, as well as related services (e.g., occupational therapy, speech therapy, transportation to a special program located away from the child's home school). These services must be fully detailed, in writing, in a document known as an Individualized Educational Plan (IEP). Specifically, an IEP must include:

- A description of the child's current level of performance.

- A description of annual goals or achievements and short-term objectives.

- A description of the specific educational and related services to be provided.

- The dates services will begin and the expected duration of each service.

- A description of the evaluation procedures used to determine whether objectives are being achieved.

The law also mandates that special education services be provided in what is known as "the least restrictive environment." In the past, handicapped children were usually segregated from nonhandicapped children in special classes or even in separate schools. Too often these special settings were little more than "dumping grounds" in which little was expected from the children in the way of achievement. Under IDEA and

its predecessor, however, handicapped children and nonhandicapped children must be educated together, to the extent that
this is possible and appropriate. For example, some youngsters
with minimally handicapping conditions can function quite
well in regular classrooms if they receive a couple of hours of
special "resource" help each week. Others simply cannot function successfully in a regular classroom setting and need the
small class size and highly specialized program and teaching
available in a self-contained classroom or school.

The school system is required to provide a continuum of
services for handicapped children, with services ranging from
special resource help for such children who can remain in the
regular classroom to residential settings for severely handicapped youngsters. If the youngster requires services that are
not available in the public school system, the school system
must pay for the child's placement in an appropriate private
facility. Nor are services available only to children who attend
public school: under IDEA, the public school system is obligated to identify and provide services to **all** children in the
school district, regardless of whether they are enrolled in public or private schools. These services include a comprehensive
evaluation as well as various support services, such as speech
therapy, occupational therapy—even consultation with personnel at the child's private school.

Finally, the law provides for parent participation in all
aspects of a child's education. Parents must, for example, give
written permission for their child to be evaluated and they
have the absolute right to review all records concerning the
child. They must also be invited to participate in developing
the IEP and they must sign it before it can be considered "offi-
cial."

ELIGIBILITY UNDER **IDEA.** A youngster diagnosed with depression is not automatically eligible for services under IDEA.
The law is quite specific: in order to qualify for services under
IDEA, a child must be determined to be in need of special
services **and** must meet criteria for one of the thirteen handi-

capping conditions covered by the law. Since there is no special category designated "depression," a depressed youngster can receive special services under IDEA only if he also satisfies the criteria applicable to one of the thirteen disability categories specified in IDEA. Depending on the findings of a multidisciplinary committee, a depressed youngster might meet criteria for one of three existing categories—"learning disabled," "seriously emotionally disturbed," or "other health-impaired."

SECTION 504

If a child does not qualify for services under IDEA, he might be eligible for services under Section 504 of the Rehabilitation Act of 1973. Eligibility requirements under this law are broader than those under IDEA: under Section 504, a person can qualify for special services if he has a physical or mental impairment which substantially limits a major life activity, such as learning.

If a depressed youngster is found to be handicapped under Section 504 and needs adjustments or accommodations in the classroom, those accommodations are required by Section 504. Examples of such accommodations include using behavior management techniques, modifying the child's work load, adjusting the child's schedule, and modifying the way in which the child is tested (e.g., untimed tests). Many of these accommodations are simply practices that skilled teachers already use to help children succeed in the classroom but, under Section 504, they must be part of a specific educational plan (much like an IEP).

HOME-SCHOOL COOPERATION

Laws can protect the rights of the child to obtain a free and appropriate education. By themselves, however, laws cannot ensure that parents and school personnel will work in har-

mony to see that the child's best interests are served. This can
be achieved only when there is a strong commitment on both
sides to avoid adversarial relationships and to work together
for the child.

When a youngster has been diagnosed with a depressive illness, one of the first questions parents usually ask is "How
much information should we share with the school?" Many
are hesitant to make this information known to school personnel: recalling the exclusionary practices that prevailed when
they were children, they fear that their child will be forever
labeled as a deviant or a misfit and that this label will haunt
him throughout his life. Parents, too, are understandably reluctant to have information about their own shortcomings or
psychiatric problems made available to teachers and others
within the school system.

     This is a delicate area and one in which a great deal of
tact must be exercised. In our own private practices, we provide parents with a full summary of our findings and recommendations concerning their youngster. Since this report is
often used to convey information to other mental health professionals such as psychiatrists and neurologists, it is imperative that all information, including personal details of family
functioning and family history, be included. When the school
system is being asked to provide very intensive levels of service, such as a self-contained program or residential care, it is
obvious that they, too, must have access to all salient information in order to provide the most helpful treatment. In the
more common case, however, in which limited services (e.g.,
accommodations in the regular classroom) are requested from
the school system, we prepare an edited version of our findings, with very personal information about the family deleted.
Parents can share this version with school personnel without

feeling embarrassed every time they attend a parent-teacher conference.

Because they see the youngster under such different circumstances, it is understandable that parents and teachers often have very different views of the depressed child or adolescent. As we noted earlier, many depressed children who are not disruptive or defiant in the school setting are irritable, demanding tyrants at home, prone to outbursts of rage and aggression when thwarted. Such children, many of whom meet criteria for a diagnosis of Oppositional Defiant Disorder, are particularly likely to be at the center of misunderstandings between parents and school personnel.

Midway through her third-grade year, Dana's parents met with her teacher, principal, and other school personnel to discuss the concerns voiced by all about Dana's poor academic performance.

"She just can't seem to get her homework organized," her teacher reported. "Maybe if you could work with her more at home it would help. She really is a sweet child but . . ."

Dana's father interrupted. "Sweet?" he snorted. "Work with her more at home? Look, I know you mean well but you obviously don't know my daughter very well. Every night when I walk through the door, my wife is on the verge of tears after another screaming match with Dana over her homework. And it's not just homework: it starts from the time she gets out of bed in the morning and goes on all day—tantrums, tears, yelling, cursing. I think school's a big part of her problem: she's so stressed out that it's making her crazy."

An uncomfortable silence was finally broken by the

guidance counselor. "This is a side of Dana we don't see in school," she said, "so there must be more to the problem than just school pressures. Have you thought about getting some counseling for the family?"

"So now you're saying it's our fault?" the father demanded. "I don't think so. I think it's you people who need to make some changes."

When the meeting ended a few minutes later, tempers on both sides were obviously frayed. Nothing had been resolved—but battle lines had been clearly drawn!

A WORKING ALLIANCE

How can parents and teachers avoid the trap of mutual blame and mistrust? To teachers, we offer the following suggestions:

- Respect the parent's knowledge and understanding of the child. Certainly, you are an expert in the area of education, but the parent is an expert on his child as a person and an individual. By encouraging the parent to talk about the child's strengths and weaknesses, likes and dislikes, you can gain information that will help you as you work with the child.

- Put yourself in the parent's shoes. Remember that the parent has a tremendous emotional investment in the child and that he or she will have responsibility for the child's care and well-being long after the child has left your classroom. Because parents have so much at stake, they are often understandably anxious. When emotions run high, people can become defensive—even belligerent. If this happens, try not to take it personally.

- Be tactful and diplomatic. If you express recognition and appreciation for the child's strengths, it makes it much easier for parents to hear you when you describe the child's weaknesses. And be careful in your choice of

words: don't use terms like "lazy" or "careless" or "unmotivated." Instead, a better approach is to ask the
parents how you can work together to help the child.
Questions phrased as "What can **we** do to . . . ?" are
more apt to open the door to communication and cooperation than challenges such as "What are **you** going to
do to . . . ?"

- Be patient with parents who seem somewhat "scat
  tered" or who have difficulty following through on
  things. Remember that parents, like the rest of us, do
  the very best they can with the resources available to
  them at the time. Remember, too, that many parents of
  depressed youngsters already feel overwhelmed by the
  special needs of their children and that many are also
  facing these demands while trying to cope with their
  own depressive illnesses.

Parents must also do their share to build a working alliance on behalf of their child. To parents, we offer these point-
ers:

- Don't ask for the impossible. As an advocate for your
  child, you certainly must insist that he receive the special services he needs to be successful in school. You
  must, however, be realistic in your demands on the
  teacher. Asking that the teacher complete a brief home-
  school checklist on a daily or weekly basis is a reason-
  able request; asking for a daily telephone consultation
  is not.

- When problems arise, be slow to draw conclusions
  about who did what and to whom. Since depressed
  youngsters tend to see the world through mud-colored
  glasses, it is likely that your child's report about altercations in the school setting may not be a completely accurate, unbiased account of what actually took place.
  While you should always accept and understand your

child's **feelings** about the incident, don't take action
without consulting the teacher and others in responsible positions. Listen carefully to their account of the
incident in question and try to withhold judgment until
you have heard their account of the situation.

• Remember that teachers—like all of us—respond to
and benefit from feedback. Take the time to express
your appreciation, not just in your thoughts but in your
actions. If you feel like sending the teacher a little bou-
quet, act on your impulse. Even better, put your feelings into written form: a note expressing your appreciation will always be warmly received, especially if you
send a copy to the principal!

TEN

What Lies Ahead?

Our Children's Future

AS YOU HAVE READ in the preceding chapters, childhood depression is a debilitating and potentially life-threatening illness. Symptoms such as boredom, irritability, inability to feel pleasure, fatigue, and changes in appetite and sleep patterns might have been overlooked or written off as "going through a phase" just a few short years ago. Today we recognize these problems as hallmarks of a mood disorder and we know that they have serious implications for a child's well-being, not only in the present, but for long years after that child becomes an adult.

We know that the rate of depression is actually on the increase in this country and abroad. We know, too, that depression is increasing at a higher rate among younger people than among older people. But what we want to know is: why is this happening? Are we just giving birth to more depressed children than our grandparents and great-grandparents did?

Can we blame the increase in depression in the population on genetics?

We think not. As we have made clear throughout this book, we believe that nature and nurture both play a role in explaining these alarming figures.

NURTURE: THE ENVIRONMENTAL FACTORS

Until scientists master the art of genetic engineering—in itself a scary proposition!—there is little we can do to change the "nature" side of the equation. But current research suggests that we can make strides toward reducing the frequency and severity of depression in young people if we maximize our efforts on the "nurture" side. Four factors seem to be particularly relevant in this regard: poverty, victimization, family dysfunction, and the expectations our society holds for its young people.

POVERTY

During the past three decades the percentage of children in the United States living below the poverty line has actually increased: in 1960, about 14 percent of children were classified as below the poverty line, in contrast to almost 22 percent in 1991 (the latest year for which we have figures).[1] There is overwhelming evidence that economic hardship in families has adverse effects on the emotional well-being of all family members; on the quality of relationships within the family; and on the availability of parents to nurture their children during critical developmental periods.[2] The quality of parenting children receive and the general conditions of their physical environment are key ingredients in their health and in their emotional development.[3] Poverty forces parents to struggle to survive, creates stress and frustration within the family, and results in a lack of parental availability and of a stimulating and nurturing environment. Poverty, in short, increases familial stress and contributes to the feelings of depression in parents and children alike.

VICTIMIZATION

Children are more likely to be victims of many types of violence than are adults. Rates of assault, rape, and robbery against teenagers, for example, are two to three times higher than for the adult population.[4]

When we look at incidents of family violence, which are not included in these figures, again we see that children fare worse than adults. While spousal abuse is all too frequent in this country, children are almost twice as likely to be the object of an adult family member's rage as are adult partners.[5] We must also consider the prevalence of peer and sibling physical abuse and assault, which is even more striking, as we discussed in Chapter 8.

Not surprisingly, there is a growing body of research literature which documents the relationship between victimization and grave short- and long-term effects on children's mental health. Children who have been sexually victimized, for example, appear to be nearly three times more likely than others to suffer from substance abuse and four times more likely to suffer an emotional disorder.[6] There is every reason to expect a relationship between child victimization and childhood depression.

FAMILY DYSFUNCTION

Parental absence has been identified as one of the most significant sources of stress and emotional disorders in childhood.[7] Parental absence at one extreme can take the form of actual abandonment or the child being orphaned. For example, approximately one hundred million children and adolescents are growing up without parents on the streets of large cities worldwide.[8] But absence can also be defined as lack of avail-

188 Lonely, Sad and Angry

ability and failure to provide the emotional, physical, and financial support critical to the good development of children, and to combat the risk of developing depression.

Children who suffer from abuse and neglect are more likely than others to end up running away and living on the streets. Even if children remain in the home, the actions of abusive and neglectful parents can create an atmosphere conducive to the development of severe emotional problems, including depression.[9]

SOCIETAL EXPECTATIONS

As a society, we certainly seem to expect more from our children today than we did in years past. Aware of the fierce competition in the job market and on the social scene, we want our children to excel, not just academically, but in all other respects as well. To meet these expectations, we may "hurry" our children, expecting them to grow up too fast and too soon.

As Tufts University professor David Elkind[10] points out, our well-meant efforts to prepare our children for successful adulthood may backfire. Our intentions, though noble, may be ill-timed, unrealistically demanding, and stress-inducing. In "hurrying" our children, we may expose them to situations that are beyond their emotional, behavioral, and cognitive capabilities. In an effort to prepare them for later life, we may be exacting a very dear cost.

CAN WE PREVENT DEPRESSION?

We know that the factors described above are related to the increase in childhood depression. We also know that we can't just wave a magic wand and have them all go away.

A more fruitful approach to preventing depression in young people might be to ask why it is that some children, despite exposure to these factors, do **not** succumb to depression and related ailments. In the face of almost overwhelming odds, why do some youngsters still function reasonably well during adolescence and as adults?

A long-term study, begun in 1955 on the Hawaiian island of Kauai, suggests some answers. This project, in which all children born on the island that year have been followed for forty years, indicates that, for almost every biological risk factor faced by a child, the outcome depended on family variables. These results strongly suggest that **what goes on within the family** can moderate and even override **what goes on within the child.**

These findings are encouraging because they highlight the importance of the one factor over which we, as parents, have some real control: the family. Just as forces within the family can contribute to the onset and maintenance of mood disorders in young people, these same forces can also be powerful agents for preventing and treating childhood depression.

HOPE FOR THE FUTURE

Despite the grim statistics we have cited in this book—statistics which seem to foretell ever increasing rates of depression in generations to come—we believe that there is hope for the future. As this book goes to press, there is a groundswell of professional and public interest in childhood depression. In the few short years since the scientific community acknowledged the existence of the condition, tremendous leaps have been made in our ability to recognize it, understand it, and treat it. In laboratories and research centers across the United States and abroad, exciting research projects are under way which promise to throw further light on questions concerning cause, treatment, and prevention.

Growing awareness of the problems of depressed children and adolescents is also indicated by the explosive growth of family advocacy and support associations such as the National

Alliance for the Mentally Ill (NAMI) and its branch, the Children and Adolescent Network (NAMI-CAN).*

This organization advocates for people with neurobiological disorders such as depression by increasing public awareness, providing information and support to families, and working to change public policy. NAMI was founded fourteen years ago by a handful of parents. Since then it has become a national organization with more than 140,000 members and over 1,000 affiliates across the United States.

Certainly, then, there is reason for optimism. In fact, we believe that more effective treatments for childhood depression are on the horizon. In the interim, parents must serve as the advance guard in the battle, since it is parents who have the responsibility for meeting the special needs of these children and advocating to see that their needs are met in the community. We recognize that this is an enormous responsibility which requires substantial investments of time, effort, caring, and commitment.

To these parents—and to the dedicated researchers who pursue knowledge to help our children—we extend our admiration and our warmest wishes.

BARBARA INGERSOLL
SAM GOLDSTEIN

---

* For information about NAMI-CAN, write to them at 2101 Wilson Boulevard, Suite 30, Arlington, VA 22201, or call them at 1-703-524-7600. For other sources of help, see Appendix B.

APPENDIX A
CHILDHOOD HISTORY FORM

Child's Name _____

Birth Date _____ Age _____ Sex _____

Home Address _____
                              Street   City
_____ Home Phone _____
          State   Zip   Area Code
Child's School _____
                          Name   Address
Grade_____ Special Placement (if any) _____

Child is presently living with:

___ Natural   ___ Natural   ___ Stepmother   ___ Stepfather
    Mother   Father
___ Adoptive   ___ Adoptive   ___ Foster   ___ Foster
    Mother   Father   Mother   Father
___ Other   _____
    (Specify)

Non-residential adults involved with this child on a regular basis

_____
_____

Source of Referral: Name _____
Address _____ Phone _____

Briefly state main problem of this child: _____
_____
_____
_____
_____

PARENTS
   Mother _____
   Occupation _____ Bus. Phone _____

Age _____ Age at time of pregnancy with patient _____

School: Highest grade completed _____
         Learning problems _____
         Attention problems _____
         Behavior problems _____

Medical Problems _____

Have any of your blood relatives experienced problems similar to those your child is experiencing? If so, describe: _____
_____
_____

Father _____ Age _____
Occupation _____ Bus. Phone _____

School: Highest grade completed _____
         Learning problems _____
         Attention problems _____
         Behavior problems _____

Medical Problems _____

Have any of your blood relatives experienced problems similar to those your child is experiencing? If so, describe: _____
_____
_____

SIBLINGS
       Name   *Age*   *Medical, Social or School Problems*
   1. _____
   2. _____
   3. _____
   4. _____
   5. _____
   6. _____

PREGNANCY—Complications

Excessive vomiting _____hospitalization required _____
Excessive staining/blood loss ___threatened miscarriage _____
Infection(s) (specify) _____
Toxemia _____Operation(s) (specify) _____
Other illness(es) (specify) _____
Smoking during pregnancy _____ #cigarettes per day _____
Alcoholic consumption during pregnancy _____
    Describe if beyond an occasional drink _____
Medications taken during pregnancy _____
X-ray studies during pregnancy _____
Duration of pregnancy (weeks) _____

DELIVERY

Type of Labor: Spontaneous ___Induced ___Duration (hrs.) _____
Type of Delivery: Normal _____ Breech _____ Caesarean _____
Complications: Cord around neck _____ Hemorrhage _____
    Infant injured during delivery _____Other _____
    Birth Weight _____

POST DELIVERY PERIOD

Jaundice _____ Cyanosis (turned blue)   Incubator Care _____
Infection (specify) _____
Number of days infant was in the hospital after delivery _____

INFANCY PERIOD

Were any of the following present—to a significant degree—during
the first few years of life? If so, describe:

    Did not enjoy cuddling _____
    Was not calmed by being held or stroked _____
    Difficult to comfort _____
    Colic _____ Excessive restlessness _____
    Excessive irritability _____
    Diminished sleep _____
    Frequent head banging _____
    Difficult nursing _____
    Constantly into everything _____

TEMPERAMENT

Please rate the following behaviors as your child appeared during infancy and toddlerhood:

Activity Level—How active has your child been from an early age? _____

_____

Distractibility—How well did your child pay attention? _____

_____

Adaptability—How well did your child deal with transition and change? _____

_____

Approach/Withdrawal—How well did your child respond to new things (i.e., places, people, food, etc.)? _____

_____

Intensity—Whether happy or unhappy, how aware are others of your child's feelings? _____

_____

Mood—What was your child's basic mood? _____

_____

Regularity—How predictable was your child in patterns of sleep, appetite, etc.? _____

_____

MEDICAL HISTORY

If your child's medical history includes any of the following, please note the age when the incident or illness occurred and any other pertinent information:

Childhood diseases (describe ages and any complications) _____

_____

Operations _____
Hospitalization for illness _____

_____

Head injuries _____
Convulsions _____ with fever _____ without fever _____
Coma _____
Persistent high fevers _____
Eye problems _____

Tics (i.e., eye blinking, sniffing, any repetitive, non-purposeful movements) _____

Ear problems _____

Allergies or Asthma _____

Poisoning _____

Sleep

Does your child settle down to sleep? _____

Sleep through the night without disruption? _____

Experience nightmares, night terrors, sleep walking, sleep talking? _____

Is your child a very restless sleeper? _____

Does your child snore? _____

Appetite _____

PRESENT MEDICAL STATUS

Height _____ Weight _____

Present illnesses for which the child is being treated _____

_____

Medications child is taking on ongoing basis _____

_____

DEVELOPMENTAL MILESTONES

If you can recall, record the age at which your child reached the following developmental milestones. If you cannot recall exactly, check item at right:

	Age	*Early*	*Normal*	*Late*
Smiled				
Sat without support				
Crawled				
Stood without support				
Walked without assistance				
Spoke first words				
Said phrases				
Said sentences				
Bladder trained, day				
Bladder trained, night				
Bowel trained, day				
Bowel trained, night				

	Age	Early	Normal	Late
Rode tricycle				
Rode bicycle (without training wheels)				
Buttoned clothing				
Tied shoelaces				
Named colors				
Named coins				
Said alphabet in order				
Began to read				

COORDINATION

Rate your child on the following skills:

	Good	Average	Poor
Walking			
Running			
Throwing			
Catching			
Shoelace tying			
Buttoning			
Writing			
Athletic abilities			
Excessive number of accidents compared to other children			

COMPREHENSION AND UNDERSTANDING

Do you consider your child to understand directions and situations as well as other children his or her age? If not, why not? _____

How would you rate your child's overall level of intelligence compared to other children?
Below Average _____ Above Average _____ Average _____

SCHOOL HISTORY

Were you concerned about your child's ability to succeed in kindergarten? If so, please explain: _____

Rate your child's school experiences related to *academic learning:*

	Good	Average	Poor
Nursery school			
Kindergarten			
Current grade			

To the best of your knowledge, at what grade level is your child functioning:

Reading _____ Spelling _____ Arithmetic _____

Has your child ever had to repeat a grade? If so, when? _____

Present class placement: Regular Class _____ Special Class (if so, specify) _____

Kinds of special counseling or remedial work your child is currently receiving _____

Describe briefly any academic school problems _____

Rate your child's school experiences related to *behavior:*

	Good	Average	Poor
Nursery school			
Kindergarten			
Current grade			

Does your child's teacher describe any of the following as significant classroom problems?

Doesn't sit still in his or her seat _____

Frequently gets up and walks around the classroom _____

Shouts out. Doesn't wait to be called on _____

Won't wait his or her turn _____

Doesn't cooperate well in group activities _____

Typically does better in a one-to-one relationship _____

Doesn't respect the rights of others _____

Doesn't pay attention during storytelling or show and tell _____

Describe briefly any *other* classroom behavioral problems _____

As best you can recall, please use the following space to provide a general description of your child's school progress in each grade. Use the back of this form if extra space is needed.

_____
_____
_____
_____
_____
_____

PEER RELATIONSHIPS

Does your child seek friendships with peers? _____
Is your child sought by peers for friendship? _____
Does your child play with children primarily his or her own age? __
   Younger? _____ Older? _____
Describe briefly any problems your child may have with peers ____

_____
_____
_____
_____

HOME BEHAVIOR

All children exhibit, to some degree, the behaviors listed below. Check those that you believe your child exhibits to an excessive or exaggerated degree when compared to other children his or her own age:

   Fidgets with hands, feet or squirms in seat _____
   Has difficulty remaining seated when required to do so _____
   Easily distracted by extraneous stimulation _____
   Has difficulty awaiting his turn in games or group situations ____
   Blurts out answers to questions before they have been
   completed _____
   Has problems following through with instructions (usually not
   due to opposition or failure to comprehend) _____
   Has difficulty paying attention during tasks or play activities ____
   Shifts from one uncompleted activity to another _____
   Has difficulty playing quietly _____

Often talks excessively _____

Interrupts or intrudes on others (often not purposeful or planned but impulsive) _____

Does not appear to listen to what is being said _____

Loses things necessary for tasks or activities at home _____

Boundless energy and poor judgment _____

Impulsivity (poor self-control) _____

History of temper tantrums _____

Temper outbursts _____

Frustrates easily _____

Sloppy table manners _____

Sudden outbursts of physical abuse of other children _____

Acts like he or she is driven by a motor _____

Wears out shoes more frequently than siblings _____

Excessive number of accidents _____

Doesn't seem to learn from experience _____

Poor memory _____

A "different child" _____

How well does your child work for a short-term reward? _____

How well does your child work for a long-term reward? _____

Does your child create more problems, either purposeful or non-purposeful, within the home setting than his or her siblings? _____
_____

Does your child have difficulty benefitting from his experiences? __
_____

Types of discipline you use with your child _____
_____
_____

Is there a particular form of discipline that has proven effective? __
_____

Have you participated in a parenting class or obtained other forms of information concerning discipline and behavior management? __
_____

INTERESTS AND ACCOMPLISHMENTS

What are your child's main hobbies and interests? _____
_____

What are your child's areas of greatest accomplishment? _____
_____

What does your child enjoy doing most? _____
_____

What does your child dislike doing most? _____
_____

What do you like about your child? _____
_____

LIST NAMES AND ADDRESSES OF ANY OTHER PROFESSIONALS CONSULTED:
(Including family doctor)

1. _____
2. _____
3. _____
4. _____

APPENDIX B
WHERE TO GET HELP

American Psychiatric Association
(202) 682-6069

American Psychological Association
(202) 336-5700

National Alliance for the Mentally Ill (NAMI)
(800) 950-NAMI

NAMI-Children and Adolescent Network
(703) 524-7600

National Depressive and Manic Depressive Association
(800) 82N-DMDA

National Foundation for Depressive Illness
(800) 248-4344

National Institute of Mental Health
Depression Awareness Campaign
(800) 421-4211

U. S. Department of Health and Human Services
"Depression Is a Treatable Disease" Brochure
(#AHCPR 93-0553) (800) 358-9295

If you would like to learn more about childhood depression, Dr. Goldstein's two-hour video "Why Isn't My Child Happy?" provides information on the causes of depression, warning signs, the process of diagnosis, proven and unproven treatments, and guidelines to assist parents, educators, and professionals. The video includes interviews with men and women on the street, families, depressed youths, and a round-table discussion. The video is available for $49.95 per copy plus $3.50 for shipping and handling from The Neurology, Learning and Behavior Center, 230 South 500 East, Suite 100, Salt Lake City, UT 84102. (801) 532-1484. FAX (801) 532-1486.

APPENDIX C
A FUN THINGS TO DO SCHEDULE*

Below is a list of things kids find fun to do. Circle all the ones that sound as if they might be fun for you. Then list the five that you think would be the most fun.

Taking a walk

Roller blading

Swimming

Jogging

Watching a movie (going to a movie)

Listening to music

Visiting with friends

Playing a game

Cooking

Reading

Going to the library

Going to a mall (going shopping)

Writing a letter

Playing a board game

Going for a drive

Having an overnight with a friend

Going out to eat

Building a model

Learning to do something new

Going to a museum or exhibit

Having friends come to visit

Spending money

Going to school

Dancing

Fishing

Playing video games

Having a party

Skateboarding

Drawing, painting, or art

Taking pictures

Planning a trip

Going to a concert

Playing golf

Playing chess or checkers

Going bowling

Receiving a gift

Giving a gift

Telling jokes

Hiking

Going to the park

Taking a bicycle ride

Playing Frisbee

* Adapted from Cautella, J. R., Cautella, J., and Esonis, S. *Forms for behavior analysis for children.* Champaign, IL: Research Press, 1983; Clarizio, H. F. *Towards Positive Classroom Discipline.* 2nd ed. New York, NY: John Wiley and Sons, 1980; and a Reinforcement Menu developed by Dr. Goldstein.

Planning something to help   Staying up late
  someone

FIVE THINGS THAT WOULD BE THE MOST FUN:

1. _____

2. _____

3. _____

4. _____

5. _____

APPENDIX D
DEPRESSION SYMPTOM CHECKLIST

Child's Name _____ Age _____ Date _____

Name of Person Completing Form _____

Relationship to Child _____

Please rate every item below by placing the number of the most descriptive statement in the box opposite each item as you have observed them for this child in the past four weeks. The five descriptive statements are:

1   You have not noticed this behavior at all.

2   You have noticed this behavior just slightly.

3   You have noticed this behavior considerably.

4   You have noticed this behavior every day.

5   You have noticed this behavior multiple times per day.

☐   This child appears unhappy, sad, down.

☐   This child makes statements suggesting hopelessness (e.g., nothing will ever help).

☐   This child seems to feel excessively guilty when something goes wrong or mistakes are made.

☐   This child appears angry and explosive.

☐   This child appears to have low self-esteem.

☐   This child blames others for any and all of his problems.

☐   This child reports suicidal thoughts.

☐   This child makes suicidal statements.

☐   This child reports that no one likes or loves him.

☐   This child seems irritable and sullen.

☐   This child does not demonstrate very much emotion.

☐   This child cries excessively over minor events.

☐   This child is isolated from peers and/or family members.

☐   This child's schoolwork has deteriorated.

☐   This child complains of frequent aches or pains.

☐   This child complains of fatigue.

☐   This child is easily agitated and upset.

☐   This child appears to lack energy.

☐   This child has fallen asleep in class.

☐   This child has a poor appetite.

☐   This child does not concentrate very well.

☐   This child complains others pick on him.

☐   This child appears easily satisfied with poor performance.

☐   This child appears to worry excessively.

☐   This child appears tense.

☐   This child appears nervous.

☐   Over the last four weeks, this child's behavior and emotional status has in general deteriorated.

Notes

Chapter One

1. Myers, J. K., Weissman, M. M., Tischler, G. L., Holzer, C. E., Leaf, P. J., Orvaschel, H., Anthony, J. C., Boyd, J. H., Burke, J. D., Kramer, M., and Stoltzman, R. "Six-month prevalence of psychiatric disorders in three communities," *Archives of General Psychiatry,* 11984, 41, 959–67.

2. National Institute of Mental Health. *Depression: What You Need to Know.* U. S. Department of Health and Human Services Publication No. ADM 87-1543, 1987.

3. American Psychiatric Association. *Diagnostic and Statistical Manual of Mental Disorders,* 4th ed. Washington, D.C., 1994.

4. Stark, K. *Childhood Depression: School-Based Intervention.* New York: Guilford Press, 1990.

5. Rosenthal, N. E. *Winter Blues: Seasonal Affective Disorder—What It Is and How to Overcome It.* New York: Guilford Press, 1993.

6. Kovacs, M., Akiskal, H. S., Gatsonis, C., and Parrone, P. L. "Childhood-onset dysthymic disorder: Clinical features and prospective naturalistic outcome," *Archives of General Psychiatry,* 1994, 51, 365–74.

7. Ibid.

8. Ferro, T., Carlson, G. A., Grayson, P., and Klein, D. N. "Depressive disorders: Distinctions in children," *Journal of the American Academy of Child and Adolescent Psychiatry,* 1994, 33, 664–70.

9. Kovacs, M., and Gatsonis, C. "Stability and change in childhood-onset depressive disorders: Longitudinal course as a diagnostic validator." In *The Validity of Psychiatric Diagnosis,* eds. L. N. Robins and J. E. Barrett. New York: Raven Press, 1989, pp. 57–76.

10. Winokur, G., Coryell, W., Endicott, J., and Akiskal, H. "Further distinctions between manic-depressive illness (bipolar disorder) and primary depressive disorder (unipolar depression)," *American Journal of Psychiatry,* 1993, 150, 1176–81.

11. Akiskal, H., Parks, W., Puzantian, V. R., King, D., Rosenthal, T. L., and

Dranon, M. "Bipolar outcome in the course of depressive illness," *Journal of Affective Disorders*, 1983, 5, 115–28.

12. Spitz, R. "Anaclitic depression," *Psychoanalytic Study of the Child*, 1946, 2, 313–42.

13. Kashani, J., Holcomb, W. R., and Orvaschel, H. "Depression and depressive symptoms in preschool children from the general population," *American Journal of Psychiatry*, 1986, 143, 1138–43.

14. McCauley, E., Carlson, G. A., and Calderone, R. "The role of somatic complaints in the diagnosis of depression in children and adolescents," *Journal of the American Academy of Child Psychiatry*, 1991, 30, 631–35.

15. Ryan, N. D., Puig-Antich, J., Ambrosini, P., Rabinovich, H., Robinson, D., Nelson, B., Iyengar, S., and Twomey, J. "The clinical picture of major depression in children and adolescents," *Archives of General Psychiatry*, 1987, 44, 854–61.

16. Offer, D. "The mystery of adolescence." In *Adolescent Psychiatry: Developmental and Clinical Studies*, Vol. 14, ed. S. C. Feinstein. Chicago: University of Chicago Press, 1987, p. 24.

17. Petersen, A. C., Kennedy, R. E., and Sullivan, P. "Coping with adolescence." In *Adolescent Stress: Causes and Consequences*, eds. M. E. Colten and S. Gore. New York: Aldine de Gruyter, 1991, 93–110.

18. Goleman, D. "Childhood depression may herald adult ills," *New York Times*, 1/11/94.

19. Kovacs, M., et al. Op. cit.

20. Lewinsohn, P. M., Hops, H., Roberts, R. E., Seeley, J. R., and Andrews, J. A. "Adolescent psychopathology: I. Prevalence and incidence of depression in other DSM III-R disorders in high school students," *Journal of Abnormal Psychology*, 1993, 102, 133–44.

21. Crystal, D. D., Chen, C., Fuligni, A., Stevenson, H. W., Shu, C., Ko, H., Kitamura, S., and Kimura, S. "Psychological maladjustment and academic achievement: a cross-cultural study of Japanese, Chinese, and American high school students," *Child Development*, 1994, 65, 738–53.

22. Coryell, W., Endicott, J., and Keller, M. "Major depression in a nonclinical sample: Demographic and clinical risk factors for first onset," *Archives of General Psychiatry*, 1992, 49, 117–25.

23. Ryan, N. D., Williamson, D. E., Iyengar, S., Orvaschel, H., Reich, T., Dahl, R. E., and Puig-Antich, J. "A secular increase in child and adolescent onset affective disorder," *Journal of the American Academy of Child and Adolescent Psychiatry*, 1992, 31, 600–5.

Chapter Two

1. Compas, B. E., Ey, S., and Grant, K. E. "Taxonomy, assessment, and diagnosis of depression during adolescence," *Psychological Bulletin*, 1993, 114, 323–44.

2. Kovacs, M., Feinberg, T. L., Crouse-Novak, M. A., Paulauskas, S. L., and Finkelstein, R. "Depressive disorders in childhood. I. A longitudinal prospective

study of characteristics and recovery," *Archives of General Psychiatry,* 1984, 41, 229–37. Kovacs, M., Feinberg, T. L., Crouse-Novak, M., Paulauskas, S. L., Pollock, M., and Finkelstein, R. "Depressive disorders in childhood. II. A longitudinal study of the risk for a subsequent major depression," *Archives of General Psychiatry,* 1984, 41, 643–49.

3. Regier, D. A., Boyd, J. H., Burke, J. D., Rae, D. S., Myers, J. K., Kramer, M., Robins, L. N., Georgia, L. K., Karno, M., and Locke, B. Z. "One-month prevalence of mental disorders in the United States: Based on five epidemiologic catchment area sites," *Archives of General Psychiatry,* 1988, 45, 977–86.

4. Kovacs, M., Gatsonis, C., Paulauskas, S. L., and Richards, C. "Depressive disorders in childhood. IV. A longitudinal study of comorbidity with and risk for anxiety disorders," *Archives of General Psychiatry,* 1989, 46, 776–82.

5. Kovacs, M., et al. Ibid.

6. McCauley, E., Myers, K., Mitchell, J., Calderon, R., Schloredt, K., and Treder, R. "Depression in young people: Initial presentation and clinical course," *Journal of the American Academy of Child and Adolescent Psychiatry,* 1993, 32, 714–22.

7. Bernstein, G. A. "Anxiety disorders," in Garfinkel, B. D., Carlson, G. A., and Weller, E. B., eds., *Psychiatric Disorders in Children and Adolescents.* Philadelphia: W. B. Saunders Co., 1990.

8. Flament, M. F., Whitaker, A., Rapoport, J. L., Davies, M., Berg, C. Z., Kalikow, K., Sceery, W., and Shaffer, D. "Obsessive compulsive disorder in adolescence: an epidemiological study," *Journal of the American Academy of Child and Adolescent Psychiatry,* 1988, 27, 764–71.

9. Robins, L. N. *Deviant Children Grown Up: A Sociological and Psychiatric Study of Sociopathic Personality.* Baltimore: Williams and Wilkins, 1966.

10. Ibid., "Sturdy childhood predictors of adult antisocial behavior: Replications from longitudinal studies," *Psychological Medicine,* 1978, 8, 611–22.

11. Ryan, N. D., Puig-Antich, J., Ambrosini, P., Rabinovich, D., Robinson, D., Nelson, B., Iyengar, S., and Twomey, J. "The clinical picture of major depression in children and adolescents," *Archives of General Psychiatry,* 1987, 44, 854–61.

12. Ferro, T., Carlson, G. A., Grayson, P., Klein, D. N. "Depressive disorders: Distinctions in children," *Journal of the American Academy of Child and Adolescent Psychiatry,* 1994, 33, 664–70.

13. Frick, P. J., Lahey, B. B., Loeber, R., Stouthamer-Lober, M., Christ, M. A., and Hanson, K. "Familial risk factors to oppositional defiant disorder and conduct disorder: Parental psychopathology and maternal parenting," *Journal of Consulting and Clinical Psychology,* 1992, 60, 49–55.

14. Mednick, S. A., Gabrielli, W. F., and Hutchings, B. "Genetic influences in criminal convictions: Evidence from an adoption cohort," *Science,* 1984, 224, 891–94.

15. Barkley, R. *Attention Deficit Hyperactivity Disorder.* New York: Guilford Press, 1990.

16. Pennington, B. F. *Diagnosing Learning Disorders: A Neuropsychological Framework.* New York: Guilford Press, 1991.

17. Wright-Strawderman, C., and Watson, B. L.. "The prevalence of depressive symptoms in children with learning disabilities," *Journal of Learning Disabilities*, 1992, 25, 258–64.

18. Rourke, B. P. *Nonverbal Learning Disabilities: The Syndrome and the Model.* New York: Guilford Press, 1989.

Chapter Three

1. Harrington, R. *Depressive Disorder in Childhood and Adolescence.* New York: John Wiley & Sons, 1993, p. 38.

2. Janicak, P. G., Davis, J. M., Preskorn, S. H., and Ayd, F. J. *Principles and Practice of Psychopharmacotherapy.* Baltimore: Williams and Wilkins, 1993, p. 16.

3. Harrington, R. Op. cit., p. 142.

4. Puig-Antich, J. "Psychobiological markers: Effects of age and puberty," in M. Rutter, C. E. Izard, and P. B. Reads, eds., *Depression in Young People: Developmental and Clinical Perspectives.* New York: Guilford Press, 1986, pp. 341–82.

5. Teicher, M. H., Glod, C. A., Harper, D., Magnus, E., Brasher, C., Wren, F., and Pahlavan, K. "Locomotor activity in depressed children and adolescents: I. Circadian dysregulation," *Journal of the American Academy of Child and Adolescent Psychiatry*, 1993, 32, 760–69.

6. Gordon Systems, Inc. P. O. Box 746, DeWitt, NY 13214.

7. Universal Attention Disorders, Inc. 4281 Katella, #215, Los Alamitos, CA 90720.

8. Multi-Health Systems, Inc., 908 Niagara Falls Boulevard, North Tonawanda, NY 14120-2060.

9. Ibid.

10. Reynolds, W. M. Reynolds Adolescent Depression Scale. Odessa, FL: Psychological Assessment Resource, Inc., 1987.

Chapter Four

1. Forward, S. *Toxic Parents: Overcoming Their Hurtful Legacy and Reclaiming Your Life.* New York: Bantam Books, 1989.

2. King, C. A., Segal, H. G., Naylor, M., and Evans, T. "Family functioning and suicidal behavior in adolescent inpatients with mood disorders," *Journal of the American Academy of Child and Adolescent Psychiatry*, 1993, 32, 1198–1206.

3. Stark, K. D., Humphrey, L. L., Crook, K., and Lewis, K. "Perceived family environments of depressed and anxious children: Child's and maternal figure's perspectives," *Journal of Abnormal Child Psychology*, 1990, 18, 527–47.

4. Ibid. Puig-Antich, J., Lukens, E., Davies, M., Goetz, D., Brennan-Quattrock, J., and Todak, G. "Psychosocial functioning in prepubertal major depressive disorders. I. Interpersonal relationships during the depressive episode," *Archives of General Psychiatry*, 1985, 42, 500–7. Puig-Antich, J., Kaufman, J., Ryan, N. D., Williamson, D. E., Dahl, R. E., Lukens, E., Todak, G., Ambrosini,

P., Rabinovich, H., and Nelson, B. "The psychosocial functioning and family environment of depressed adolescents," *Journal of the American Academy of Child and Adolescent Psychiatry,* 1993, 32, 244–53.

5. Forehand, R., McCombs, A., and Brody, G. H. "The relationship between parental depressive mood states and child functioning," *Advances in Behavior Therapy and Research,* 1987, 9, 1–20.

6. Cox, A. D., Puckering, C., Pound, A., and Mills, M. "The impact of maternal depression in young people," *Journal of Child Psychology and Psychiatry,* 1987, 28, 917–28.

7. Abramson, L. Y., Seligman, M. E. P., and Teasdale, J. D. "Learned helplessness in humans: Critique and reformulation," *Journal of Abnormal Psychology,* 1978, 87, 49–74.

8. Reinherz, H. Z., Giaconia, R. M., Pakiz, B., Silverman, A. B., Frost, A. K., and Lefkowitz, E. S. "Psychosocial risks for major depression in adolescence: A longitudinal community study," *Journal of the American Academy of Child and Adolescent Psychiatry,* 1993, 32, 1155–63.

9. Pine, D., Shaffer, D., and Schonfeld, I. S. "Persistent emotional disorder in children with neurological soft signs," *Journal of the American Academy of Child and Adolescent Psychiatry,* 1993, 32, 1229–36.

10. Chess, S., and Thomas, A. *Origins and Evolution of Behavior Disorders: From Infancy to Early Adult Life.* New York: Brunner/Mazel, 1984.

11. Maziade, M., Caron, C., Cote, R., Boutin, P., and Thivierge, J. "Extreme temperament and diagnosis: A study in a psychiatric sample of consecutive children," *Archives of General Psychiatry,* 1990, 47, 477–84.

12. Kagan, J. "Temperamental conditioning to social behavior," *American Psychologist,* 1989, 44, 668–74.

13. Goodyer, I. M., Ashby, L., Altham, P. M. E., Vize, C., and Cooper, P. J. "Temperament and major depression in 11 to 16 year olds," *Journal of Child Psychology and Psychiatry,* 1993, 34, 1409–23.

14. Puig-Antich, J., et al. Op. cit. "I. Interpersonal relationships during the depressive episode," *Archives of General Psychiatry,* 1985, 42, 500–7; ibid. "II. Interpersonal relationships after sustained recovery from affective episode," *Archives of General Psychiatry,* 1985, 42, 511–17.

15. Bifulco, A., Brown, G. W., and Harris, T. O. "Childhood loss of parent, lack of adequate parental care and adult depression: A replication," *Journal of Affective Disorders,* 1987, 12, 115–18.

16. Koverola, C., Pound, J., Heger, A., and Lytle, C. "Relationship of child sexual abuse to depression," *Child Abuse and Neglect,* 1993, 17, 393–400.

17. Cherlin, A. J., Furstenberg, F. F., Chase-Lansdale, P. L., Kiernan, K. E., Robins, P. K., Morrison, D. R., and Teitler, J. O. "Longitudinal studies of effects of divorce on children in Great Britain and the United States," *Science,* 1991, 252, 1386–89.

18. Harrington, R. *Depressive Disorder in Childhood and Adolescence.* Chichester, England: John Wiley and Sons, 1993, p. 119.

19. Compas, B. E., Howell, D. C., Phares, V., Williams, R. A., and Ledoux,

N. "Parent and child stress and symptoms: An integrative analysis," *Developmental Psychology*, 1989, 25, 550–59.

20. Gershon, E. S., Hamovit, J., Guroff, J., Dibble, E., Leckman, J. F., Sceery, W., Targum, S. D., Nurnberger, J. I., Goldin, L. R., and Bunney, W. E. "A family study of schizoaffective, bipolar I, bipolar II, unipolar probands and normal controls," *Archives of General Psychiatry*, 1982, 39, 1157–67.

21. National Institute of Mental Health. *Depressive Illnesses: Treatments Bring New Hope*. Rockville, MD: Department of Health and Human Services Publication No. (ADM) 89-1491, 1989.

22. Mendlewicz, J., and Rainer, J. "Adoption study supporting genetic transmission in manic-depressive illness," *Nature*, 1977, 268, 327–29. Wender, P. H., Kety, S. S., Rosenthal, D., Schulsinger, F., Ortmann, J., and Lunde, I. "Psychiatric disorders in the biological and adoptive families of adopted individuals with affective disorders," *Archives of General Psychiatry*, 1986, 43, 923–29.

23. Puig-Antich, J., Goetz, D., Davies, M., Kaplan, T., Davies, S., Ostrow, L., Asnis, L., Twomey, J., Iyengar, S., and Ryan, N. D. "A controlled family history study of prepubertal major depressive disorder," *Archives of General Psychiatry*, 1989, 46, 406–18.

24. Sherrington, C. C. in Lallett, P., ed., *The Physical Basis of Mind*. New York: Macmillan, 1950.

Chapter Five

1. Rosenthal, N. E. *Winter Blues: Seasonal Affective Disorder—What It Is and How to Overcome It*. New York: Guilford Press, 1993, p. 155.

2. Ibid., p. 158.

3. Wolpe, J. *Psychotherapy by Reciprocal Inhibition*. Stanford: Stanford University Press, 1958.

4. Beck, A., Rush, A., Shaw, B., and Emery, G. *Cognitive Therapy of Depression*. New York: Guilford Press, 1979.

5. Ellis, A. *Reason and Emotion in Psychotherapy*. New York: Lyle Stuart, 1962.

6. Kempton, T., Van Hasselt, V. B., Bukstein, O. G., and Null, J. "Cognitive distortions and psychiatric diagnosis in dually diagnosed adolescents," *Journal of the American Academy of Child and Adolescent Psychiatry*, 1994, 33, 217–22.

7. Lewinsohn, P. M., Hoberman, H. M., and Clarke, G. N. "The Coping with Depression Course: Review and future directions," *Canadian Journal of Behavioral Science*, 1989, 21, 470–93.

8. Rotherman-Borus, M. J., Placentini, J., Miller, S., Graae, F., and Castro-Blanco, D. "Brief cognitive-behavioral treatment for adolescent suicide attempters and their families," *Journal of the American Academy of Child and Adolescent Psychiatry*, 1994, 33, 508–17.

9. Knell, S. M. *Cognitive-Behavioral Play Therapy*. Northvale, NJ: Jason Aronson, Inc., 1993.

10. Mufson, L., Moreau, D., Weissman, M. M., and Klerman, G. L. *Interper-

sonal Psychotherapy for Depressed Adolescents. New York: Guilford Press, 1993, p. 9.

11. Mufson, L., Moreau, D., Weissman, M. M., Wickramaratne, P., Martin, J., and Samoilov, A. "Modification of interpersonal psychotherapy with depressed adolescents (ITP-A): Phase I and II Studies," *Journal of the American Academy of Child and Adolescent Psychiatry,* 1994, 33, 695–705.

12. Harrington, R. *Depressive Disorder in Childhood and Adolescence.* Chichester, England: John Wiley and Sons, 1993, p. 161.

Chapter Six

1. Gittelman-Klein, R., and Klein, D. F. "Controlled imipramine treatment of school phobia," *Archives of General Psychiatry,* 1971, 25, 204–7.

2. Petti, T. A. "Imipramine in the treatment of depressed children," in D. P. Cantwell and G. A. Carlson, eds., *Affective Disorders in Childhood and Adolescents: An Update,* Lancaster, PA: MTP Press, 1983, 375–415.

3. Ambrosini, P. J., Metz, C., Bianchi, M., and Rabinovich, H. "Open nortriptylene treatment over 10 weeks in depressed adolescent outpatients," *Proceedings of the American Academy of Child and Adolescent Psychiatry,* 1989, 5, 59.

4. Ambrosini, P. J., Bianchi, M. D., Rabinovich, H., Elia, J. "Antidepressant treatments in children and adolescents. I. Affective disorders," *Journal of the American Academy of Child and Adolescent Psychiatry,* 1993, 32, 1–6.

5. Harrington, R. *Depressive Disorder in Childhood and Adolescence.* Chichester, England: John Wiley and Sons, 1993, p. 179.

6. Janicak, P. G., Davis, J. M., Preskorn, S. H., and Ayd, F. J. *Principles and Practice of Psychopharmacotherapy.* Baltimore: Williams and Wilkins, 1993, p. 281.

7. Reimhers, F., Wood, D., Byerley, B., Brainard, J., and Brosser, B. "Characteristics of responders to fluoxetine," *Psychopharmacology Bulletin,* 1984, 20, 70–72.

8. Jain, U., Birmaher, B., Garcia, M., Al-Shabbout, M., and Ryan, N. "Fluoxetine in children and adolescents with mood disorders: A chart review of efficacy and adverse effects," *Journal of Child and Adolescent Psychopharmacology,* 1992, 2, 259–65.

9. Boulos, C., Kutcher, S., Gardner, D., and Young, E. "An open naturalistic trial of fluoxetine in adolescents and young adults with treatment-resistant major depression," *Journal of Child and Adolescent Psychopharmacology,* 1992, 2, 103–14.

10. Apter, A., Ratzoni, G., King, R. A., Weizman, A., Iancu, J., Binder, M., and Riddle, M. A. "Fluvoxamine open-label treatment of adolescent inpatients with obsessive-compulsive disorder or depression," *Journal of the American Academy of Child and Adolescent Psychiatry,* 1994, 33, 342–48.

11. Birmaher, B., Waterman, G. S., Ryan, N., Cully, M., Balach, L., Ingram, J., and Brodsky, M. "Fluoxetine for childhood anxiety disorders," *Journal of the American Academy of Child and Adolescent Psychiatry,* 1994, 33, 993–99.

12. Black, B., and Uhde, T. W. "Treatment of elective mutism with fluoxe-

tine: A double-blind, placebo-controlled study," *Journal of the American Academy of Child and Adolescent Psychiatry*, 1993, 33, 1000–6.

13. Riddle, M. A., Scahill, L., King, R. A., Hardin, M. T., Anderson, G. M., Ort, S. I., Smith, J. C., Leckman, J. F., and Cohen, D. J. "Double-blind, crossover trial of fluoxetine and placebo in children and adolescents with Obsessive-Compulsive Disorder," *Journal of the American Academy of Child and Adolescent Psychiatry*, 1992, 31, 1062–69.

14. Mann, J., and Kapur, S. "The emergence of suicidal ideation and behavior during antidepressant pharmacotherapy," *Archives of General Psychiatry*, 1991, 48, 1027–33.

15. Alessi, N., Naylor, M. W., Ghaziuddin, M., Zubieta, J. K. "Update on lithium carbonate therapy in children and adolescents," *Journal of the American Academy of Child and Adolescent Psychiatry*, 1994, 33, 291–304.

16. Campbell, M., Small, A. M., Pardon–Gayol, M. V., Locascio, J. J., Kafantaris, V., and Overall, J. E. "Lithium in aggressive children with conduct disorder," *Clinical Neuropharmacology*, 1990b, 13, 615–16.

17. Salzman, C. "Benzodiazepine dependency: Summary of the APA task force on benzodiazepines," *Psychopharmacology Bulletin*, 1990, 26, 61–62.

18. Bernstein, G. A., Garfinkel, B. D., and Borchardt, C. M. "Comparative studies of pharmacotherapy for school refusal," *Journal of the American Academy of Child and Adolescent Psychiatry*, 1990, 29, 773–81; and Graae, F., Milner, J., Rizzotto, L., and Klein, R. G. "Clonazepam in childhood anxiety disorders," *Journal of the American Academy of Child and Adolescent Psychiatry*, 1994, 33, 372–76.

19. Kutcher, S. P., Reiter, S., Gardner, D. M., and Klein, R. G. "The pharmacotherapy of anxiety disorders in children and adolescents," *Psychiatric Clinics of North America*, 1992, 43, 62–68; and Simon, J. G., Knott, V. J., DuBois, C., Wiggens, D., Geraet, I., Thatte, S., and Miller, W. "Buspirone therapy of mixed anxiety disorders in childhood and adolescence: a pilot study," *Journal of Child and Adolescent Psychopharmacology*, 1994, 4, 159–70.

20. Simeon, J. G., and Ferguson, H. B. "Alprazolam effects in children with anxiety disorders," *Canadian Journal of Psychiatry*, 1987, 32, 570–74.

21. Gammon, G. D., and Brown, T. E. "Fluoxetine and methylphenidate in combination for treatment of Attention Deficit Disorder and comorbid depressive disorder," *Journal of Child and Adolescent Psychopharmacology*, 1993, 3, 1–10.

22. Medical Economics Company, Inc. Physicians' Desk Reference. Oradell, NJ: Edward R. Barnhart.

23. Janicak, P. G., et al., op. cit., p. 52.

24. Coffey, C. E., Weiner, R. D., Djang, W. T., Figiel, G. S., Soady, S. A. R., Patterson, L. J., Holt, P. D., Spritzer, C. E., and Wilkinson, W. E. "Brain anatomic effects of electroconvulsive therapy: A prospective magnetic resonance imaging study," *Archives of General Psychiatry*, 1991, 48, 1013–21.

25. Bertagnoli, M. W., and Broschardt, C. M. "Case study: a review of ECT for children and adolescents," *Journal of the American Academy of Child and Adolescent Psychiatry*, 1990, 29, 302–7.

26. Rosenthal, N. E., Sack, D. A., Carpenter, C. J. "Antidepressant effects of

light in seasonal affective disorder," *American Journal of Psychiatry*, 1985, 142, 163–70.

27. Sonis, W. A., Yellin, A. M., Garfinkel, B. D. "The antidepressant effect of light in seasonal affective disorder of childhood and adolescence," *Psychopharmacology Bulletin*, 1987, 23, 360–63.

Chapter Seven

1. King, C. A., Segal, H. G., Naylor, M., and Evans, T. "Family functioning and suicidal behavior in adolescent patients with mood disorders," *Journal of the American Academy of Child and Adolescent Psychiatry*, 1993, 32, 1198–1206.

2. Jennings, M., 1990. Cited in M. Shaffi and S. L. Shaffi, *Clinical Guide to Depression in Children and Adolescents*. Washington, D.C.: American Psychiatric Association Press, 1992.

3. Shaffer, D., Garland, A., Gould, M., Fisher, P., and Trautman, P. "Preventing teenage suicide: A critical review," *Journal of the American Academy of Child and Adolescent Psychiatry*, 1988, 27, 675–87.

4. Guze, S. B., and Robins, E. "Suicide and primary affective disorders," *British Journal of Psychiatry*, 1970, 117, 437–48.

5. Kutchner, S. P., and Korenblum, M. "Borderline personality disorder in adolescents: a critical overview, novel speculations, and suggested future directions," in D. Silver and M. Rosenbluth, eds., *Handbook of Borderline Personality Disorders*. Madison, CT: International Universities Press, 1992, p. 538.

6. Adams, D. M., Overholser, J. C., and Lehnert, K. L. "Perceived family functioning and adolescent suicidal behavior," *Journal of the American Academy of Child and Adolescent Psychiatry*, 1994, 33, 498–507.

7. King, C. A., et al. Op. cit.

8. Nielsen, D. A., Goldman, D., Virkkunen, M., Tokola, R., Rawlings, R., and Linnoila, M. "Suicidality and 5-hydroxyindoleacetic acid concentration associated with a tryptophan hydroxylase polymorphism," *Archives of General Psychiatry*, 1994, 51, 34–38.

9. Ibid.

10. Gibson, P. "Gay male and lesbian youth suicide," in U. S. Department of Health and Human Services, ed., *Report of the Secretary's Task Force on Youth Suicide*. Washington, D.C.: U. S. Department of Health and Human Services, 1989, 110–42.

11. Marttunen, M. J., Aro, H. M., and Lonnqvist, J. K. "Precipitant stressors in adolescent suicide," *Journal of the American Academy of Child and Adolescent Psychiatry*, 1993, 32, 1178–83.

12. Brent, D. A., Kerr, M. M., Goldstein, C., Bozigar, J., Wartella, M., and Allan, M. J. "An outbreak of suicide and suicidal behavior in a high school," *Journal of the American Academy of Child and Adolescent Psychiatry*, 1989, 28, 918–24.

13. Ibid.

14. Brent, D. A., Pepper, J., Moritz, G., Allman, C., Friend, A., Schweers, J., Roth, C., Balach, L., and Harrington, K. "Psychiatric effects of exposure to sui-

cide among the friends and acquaintances of adolescent suicide victims," *Journal of the American Academy of Child and Adolescent Psychiatry*, 1992, 31, 629–39.

15. Oster, G. D., and Caro, J. E. *Understanding and Treating Depressed Adolescents.* New York: John Wiley and Sons, 1990.

16. American Academy of Child and Adolescent Psychiatry. *Policy Statement: Inpatient hospital treatment of children and adolescents.* Washington, D.C., June 1989.

17. Patrick, C., Padgett, D. K., Burns, B. J., Schlesinger, H. J., and Cohen, J. "Use of inpatient services by a national population: Do benefits make a difference?" *Journal of the American Academy of Child and Adolescent Psychiatry*, 1993, 32, 144–52.

18. Rosenstock, H., and Vincent, K. "Parental involvement as a requisite for successful adolescent therapy," *Journal of Clinical Psychiatry*, 1979, 40, 132–34.

19. Harper, G. "Focal inpatient treatment planning," *Journal of the American Academy of Child and Adolescent Psychiatry*, 1989, 28, 31–37.

Chapter Eight

1. Taylor, J. F. *The Hyperactive Child and the Family.* New York: Dodd, Mead, 1980.

2. Merikangas, K., and Spiker, D. G. "Assortative mating among inpatients with primary affective disorder," *Psychological Medicine*, 1982, 12, 753–64.

3. Faber, A., and Mazlish, E. *Siblings Without Rivalry.* New York: Avon Books, 1987, p. 36.

4. Finkelhor, D., and Dziuba-Leatherman, J. "Victimization of children," *American Psychologist*, 1994, 49, 179–83.

5. Puig-Antich, J., Kaufman, J., Ryan, N. D., Williamson, D. E., Dahl, R. E., Lukens, E., Todak, G., Ambrosini, P., Rabinovich, H., and Nelson, B. "The psychosocial functioning and family environment of depressed adolescents," *Journal of the American Academy of Child and Adolescent Psychiatry*, 1993, 32, 244–53.

6. Dunn, J., and Kendrick, C. *Siblings: Love, Envy and Understanding.* Cambridge, MA: Harvard University Press, 1982.

7. Ames, L. B. *He Hit Me First: When Brothers and Sisters Fight.* New York: Dembner Books, 1982.

8. Cole, D. A., and Rehm, L. P. "Family interaction patterns and childhood depression," *Journal of Abnormal Child Psychology*, 1986, 14, 297–314.

9. Stark, K. D., Humphrey, L. L., Crook, K., and Lewis, K. "Perceived family environments of depressed and anxious children: Child's and maternal figure's perspectives," *Journal of Abnormal Child Psychology*, 1990, 18, 527–47.

10. Lewinsohn, P. M., and Graf, M. "Pleasant activities and depression," *Journal of Consulting and Clinical Psychology*, 1973, 41, 261–86.

11. McLean, P. D. "Therapeutic decision-making in the behavioral treatment of depression," in P. Davidson, ed., *The Behavioral Management of Anxiety, Depression, and Pain.* New York: Brunner/Mazel, 1975, 54–90.

12. Phelan, T. W. *1-2-3: Magic! Training Your Preschoolers and Preteens to*

Do What You Want. Glen Ellyn, IL: Child Management, 1984. Available from Child Management, Inc., 800 Roosevelt Road, Glen Ellyn, IL 60137.

Chapter Nine

1. Levine, M. D. *Developmental Variation and Learning Disorders.* Cambridge, MA: Educators Publishing Service, Inc., 1987, p. 2.

2. Barclay, J. R. "Effecting behavior change in the elementary school classroom: An exploratory study," *Journal of Counseling Psychology,* 1967, 14, p. 240.

3. Guevremont, D. C. "The parent's role in helping the ADHD child with peer relationships," *CH.A.D.D.ER,* 1992, 6 (2) p. 18. (Semiannual publication of Children and Adults with Attention Deficit Disorder, Plantation, FL.)

Chapter Ten

1. United States Bureau of Census. *Poverty in the United States, 1991.* Current population reports, Series P-60, #181. Washington, D.C.: U. S. Government Printing Office, 1992.

2. Conger, R. D., Ge, X., Elder, G. H., Lorenz, F. O., and Simons, R. L. "Economic stress, coercive family process, and developmental problems of adolescents," *Child Development,* 65, 1994, 541–61.

3. U. S. Department of Health and Human Services. *Health Status of Minorities in Low Income Groups.* Washington, D.C.: Government Printing Office. 1994.

4. Bureau of Justice Statistics. *Teenage victims: the national crime survey reports* (NCJ 12819). Washington, D.C.: U. S. Department of Justice, 1991.

5. Straus, M. A., and Gelles, R. J. *Physical Violence in American Families: Risk Factors and Adaptations to Violence in 8,145 Families.* New Brunswick, NJ: Transaction Press, 1990.

6. Saunders, B. E., Villeponteaux, L. A., Lipovsky, J. A., Kirkpatrick, D. G., and Veronen, L. J. "Child sexual assault as a risk factor for mental disorders among women: a community survey," *Journal of Interpersonal Violence,* 7, 1992, 189–204.

7. Arnold, L. E. *Childhood Stress.* New York: Wiley Interscience Press, 1990.

8. UNICEF. UNICEF Annual Report. New York: UNICEF, 1989.

9. Campos, R., Raffaelli, M., Ude, W., Greco, M., Ruff, A., Rolf, J., Antunes, C. M., Halsey, N., Greco, D., and The Street Youth Study Group. "Social networks and daily activities of street youth in Belo Horizonte, Brazil," *Child Development,* 65, 1994, 319–30.

10. Elkind, D. *The Hurried Child: Growing Up Too Fast Too Soon.* Reading, MA: Addison-Wesley, 1981.

Index

clusters, 129–30
"contagion effect," 129–30
family history of, 126
gender differences, 123
ideation, 44
intervention, 131–33
methods, 123–24
precipitants, 128–30
preoccupation with, 9
risk factors, 3, 124–28
statistics, 122, 124
threats of, 27
Support groups, 117–18, 189–90, 201
Systematic desensitization, 84, 85

Talkativeness, 13
Taylor, Dr. John, 148
Tegretol, 108
Temperament, 66–67, 151–52, 194
elements of, 67–68
in infancy, 68
and parent-child interactions, 69–70
and psychological problems, 68–69
Temper tantrums, 3, 4, 5, 14–15, 18, 27, 42, 85, 144
Test of Variables of Attention, 49
Tests
achievement, 48–49
Behavioral Screening questionnaire, 50
blood, 48
Child Behavior checklist, 50
Children's Depression Inventory, 50, 51
computerized tomography, 47, 120, 136
Continuous Performance Test, 49
Depression Symptom Checklist, 54, 204–15
diagnostic, 46–54
electrocardiogram, 48, 102, 136
electroencephalogram, 48, 136
Gordon Diagnostic System, 49
intelligence, 38, 48–49

magnetic resonance imaging, 47, 77n, 136
medical, 46–48
Millon Adolescent Personality Inventory, 50
Minnesota Multiphasic Personality Inventory, 50
neurological, 48
Peabody Individual Achievement Test, 49
performance, 48–49
polysomnography, 47
projective, 49–54
psychological, 48–54, 136
Revised Children's Manifest Anxiety Scale, 50, 53
Reynolds Adolescent Depression Scale, 50, 52
Rorschach Inkblot Test, 49
Test of Variables of Attention, 49
Thematic Apperception Test, 49
urine, 48
Wechsler Intelligence Scale for Children, 49
Wide Range Achievement Test, 49
Woodcock-Johnson Psychoeducational Battery, 49
Thematic Apperception Test, 49
Therapy
art, 141
behavior, 79, 82, 83–86, 154–60
billing for, 95
choosing a therapist, 93–96
cognitive, 79, 82, 84, 86–89, 148
costs of, 96–97
drawbacks of, 82–83, 89, 91, 93
effectiveness of, 82, 85–86, 89, 90, 92–93
electroconvulsive, 119–20
family, 43, 60n, 79, 90–91, 141
goals, 81
group, 89, 141
individual, 60n, 141
insight-oriented, 79, 80–83
interpersonal, 79, 91–93
light, 120–21

BARBARA INGERSOLL, PH.D., has treated hyperactive children and counseled their families for more than twenty years. She holds a Ph.D. in clinical psychology from the Pennsylvania State University. She was an associate professor at the West Virginia University School of Medicine and is now on the clinical faculty of their Department of Psychiatry and Behavioral Medicine. She is a member of the Professional Advisory Board of the parents' support group CH.A.A.D. (Children and Adults with Attention Deficit Disorders), and lives and practices in Bethesda, Maryland. She is also the author of *Your Hyperactive Child: A Parent's Guide to Coping with Attention Deficit Disorder* (Doubleday).

SAM GOLDSTEIN, PH.D., is a clinical instructor in the Department of Psychiatry at the University of Utah School of Medicine. Since 1982, Dr. Goldstein has worked in private practice as part of a multidisciplinary team, providing evaluation, case management, and treatment services for children and adults with histories of neurological disease and trauma, learning disability, adjustment difficulties, and attention deficit disorder. His parenting videos have won numerous awards, including three from the New York Film Festival. He is a member of the Professional Advisory Board for CH.A.A.D. and the author of *Managing Attention Disorders in Children* (Wiley) and *Hyperactivity: Why Won't My Child Pay Attention?* (Wiley).

Barbara Ingersoll and Sam Goldstein are also the authors of *Attention Deficit Disorder and Learning Disabilities: Realities, Myths and Controversial Treatments* (Doubleday).